MW01062028

CONGREGATIONS ALIVE

_____   .   _____

To Dorothy Siebers
with gratitude for your
service on the Board
of the Vocation Agency

Don

BOOKS BY DONALD P. SMITH
Published by The Westminster Press

Congregations Alive

*Clergy in the Cross Fire: Coping with Role Conflicts
in the Ministry*

CONGREGATIONS ALIVE

by
DONALD P. SMITH

Donald P Smith

THE WESTMINSTER PRESS
Philadelphia

BOOK DESIGN BY DOROTHY ALDEN SMITH

First edition

Published by The Westminster Press®
Philadelphia, Pennsylvania

PRINTED IN THE UNITED STATES OF AMERICA
9 8 7 6 5 4 3 2 1

Library of Congress Cataloging in Publication Data

Smith, Donald P., 1922–
   Congregations alive.

   Includes bibliographical references.
   1. Theology, Practical. I. Title.
BV3.S65   253   81–1371
ISBN 0–664–24370–3   AACR2

CONTENTS

This book is written for pastors, officers, and members of congregations who are open to a new adventure. It is for those who want to discover what the Holy Spirit can do through them when they commit themselves to becoming God's servant people in the world. It is intended to be used by congregational leaders as a stimulus to dialogue about the style and content of their leadership, and as a catalyst to prod them into new ways of working together in shared ministry. It can be studied as background for a church officers retreat, or its chapters discussed during a period set aside as part of their regular meetings.

A sound filmstrip, *A Tale of Three Churches,* has been designed to introduce the themes of this book. It is available from the Vocation Agency, The United Presbyterian Church in the United States of America, 475 Riverside Drive, New York, N.Y. 10115.

This book is not a theological treatise on ministry. It does not seek to make a contribution to the theology of the *laos,* nor to the theology of ordination. On the first, a significant consensus already exists. On the second, considerable confusion and ferment remain. Others are working at those tasks.

The study behind this book was undertaken out of my conviction that at this stage in the life of the church a greater contribution toward mutual ministry could be made by changing our way of doing things than by refining our theological formulations. Shared ministry leads to vitality. I have described how some congregations act out a genuine partnership in ministry so that others may discover their own ways to come alive.

It is clear that in the ministering congregations studied here, the pastor plays a very important role in partnership. Within the ministering congregations there are also many evidences of initiative in ministry from members and officers. If they are not as evident in the illustrations as they might be, it is because I was seeking to understand leadership styles that encourage the ministries of all church members. But more important, it is because at this stage in the life of the church, progress toward partnership demands the initiative and cooperation of the pastor.

This book deliberately accentuates the positive. Of course there are problems in all the ministering congregations. They are human too. But it is my conviction that the church spends too much energy analyzing problems. Too little attention is given to creative movements of the Spirit. Most readers will quickly identify possible pitfalls. I hope that the possibilities given here will outweigh the questions that remain.

This book is dedicated to the scores of congregations that are embarked on the servant pilgrimage and are already discovering what that journey can mean for the church of Jesus Christ in our day. In a special way it is dedicated to the particular congregations that welcomed me into the inner circles of their life, that generously helped me glimpse their vision of shared ministry, and that welcomed my inquiry into the "whys" of their life together. The warmth of their caring love has opened my eyes to the vitality that can emerge in a congregation that takes mutual ministry seriously. In some small measure, I hope I have been able to communicate that vitality in such a way that others will be eager to discover what partnership can mean to them.

Without the vision, encouragement, and generosity of the Board of the Vocation Agency of The United Presbyterian Church in the U.S.A., this book could not have been written. Because of their conviction of the crucial importance of the ministry of the whole people of God, I was released completely from my regular responsibilities and assigned to undertake the study that led to this book. The book indeed belongs to them, although I take personal responsibility for what I say.

The Office of Research of the Support Agency of our denomination worked with me to design the research instruments and to carry out the extensive analysis of voluminous data. That analysis lies behind the generalizations made in this book. Technical data have deliberately been excluded from this work, but are available from the Vocation Agency to those who are interested.

Quotations from pastors, elders, and church members used throughout the book are in their own words, cited with minor editorial revisions for literary consistency. Occasionally, statements of more than one person are combined. Fictitious names have been used both for congregations and for individuals.

The terminology used throughout may make this appear to be a Presbyterian book. It is not. Because they were available to us, the study concentrated upon Presbyterian congregations. Therefore, the terms "elders" and "session" appear frequently. However, what has been learned applies to other denominations. Simply substitute comparable terminology from your own tradition. I am confident the ideas will then be useful.

Because the book analyzes what church leaders actually do to catalyze partnership in ministry, it contains many practical possibilities for action. These must be translated and adapted to particular situations. Take what is applicable to your congregation and use it. Ministering congregations, however, exhibit a *constellation of interrelated themes.* There is an *organic* or *systemic* quality about them. To concentrate on one theme without the others may rend the tapestry of mutual ministry which has been woven here.

I am grateful to over a hundred pastors, elders, presbytery executives, seminary professors, board members, and others who have helped in the study. I am deeply indebted to the creative and hardworking staff of the Vocation Agency who insisted that I undertake the writing task, who gave constructive criticism along the way, and who voluntarily shouldered heavy additional work loads during my absence from my normal responsibilities. Finally, I pay tribute to my beloved wife, Verna, who bears patiently the absences required by my work, and who, in addition to that, endured many hours of isolation at home while the completion of this project was under way.

CHAPTER 1

A Look at Living Congregations

The Spirit of the Lord is upon me,
  because he has chosen me to bring good
    news to the poor.
He has sent me to proclaim liberty to the
    captives
  and recovery of sight to the blind,
to set free the oppressed
  and announce that the time has come
  when the Lord will save his people.
                    (Luke 4:18–19, TEV)

What gets church members involved in ministry?

It is 6:30 Tuesday morning in a comfortable suburban community. Nine men are gathered at the Garden Hills Church an hour earlier than their usual daily commuting time. As they do every week, they have come for Bible study, sharing, and prayer together. One of them has prepared juice, coffee, and doughnuts. They help themselves and quickly get down to business. The pastor of the congregation is one of them, but he does not lead the group.

During the Bible study discussion someone paraphrases Scripture: "If you love me, all I ask is that you love your brother and sister." Another says, "My loyalty to God is to reach out to the need of others as God has reached out to me, and to share what I have with them."

When the time comes for sharing, one of the group tells of a neighbor couple whose marriage is shaky. They have just lost a child. "What shall I do?" he asks. "How can I help them?" He himself has just been through a Marriage Encounter group which has given new life to his own marriage. But how can he help his friends?

A second member is dissolving his business partnership. The group asks how it is going.

Another speaks of a friend at work who is going through a second divorce. He shares what he is doing to help.

Bill requests a prayer for Pete, who has just had to put a member of his family back into a mental hospital. Pete is overwhelmed and needs support.

A social worker speaks. "I need several men who will come to the convalescent center and just be a friend to some of the lonely men who are there." "Why don't you put a notice in the church newsletter?" one of them suggests. "Maybe I could help," says Bill. The feeling is unanimous: "No, you should not get yourself involved in that. You need to concentrate on building that relationship with Pete. He needs you now."

Several of the members offer prayer. Quickly they leave to catch their buses.

Coming Alive to Ministry

How do people come alive to ministry? That is the subject of this book. The insights offered here have been gained through listening to people like those nine men, in congregations that have a high level of involvement of their members in ministry to one another and the community.

It is Thursday afternoon in the heart of a Spanish-American neighborhood in a large metropolitan area. The Christian Education building of the Saint James Church is alive with activity. A nursery school has been in session throughout the day. Now, in another section of the building, thirty to forty children are deeply involved in a number of activities under the guidance of perhaps a dozen volunteers. In several different rooms children are paired with tutors who are helping them gain a mastery of English and are giving remedial assistance in other school subjects. In a large room, several volunteers are guiding about fifteen to thirty children in craft projects and other activities aimed at developing language and socialization skills. One by one, each child leaves the room for private tutoring, and later returns.

Within a few blocks of the church building a community center staff works with young people for whom drug abuse is a major problem. Elsewhere there is a Head Start program. Not far away a youth park has just been created by the neighborhood. Members of the congregation themselves have put the roof on its recreation building.

The Saint James congregation of 275 members initiated all these community ventures. Now they are operated and supported by the entire community with state and federal funding. Members of that congregation continue to be key instruments for change in the community. They are leaders on the YMCA board, which has just conducted a successful youth gang outreach program. They are active on the boards of many other ventures. Each summer, the congregation serves about four hundred meals a day to neighborhood children. All this began several years ago when the Saint James Church, made up largely of Anglos, decided to seek to minister to its community of Chicanos. A small Spanish-speaking congregation is now worshiping in the sanctuary.

When asked why members are giving themselves to such extensive service, Mary replied, "We serve because Christ commands us to do so, and because we are a caring community to which we want them to belong."

What stimulates congregations to get involved in ministry to one another and to their communities?

A Study of Ministering Congregations

The foregoing illustrations are from 2 of the 97 congregations that participated in a study conducted by the Vocation Agency of The United Presbyterian Church in the U.S.A. The congregations were selected because they demonstrated partnership in ministry between pastor and people and because their members were deeply involved in service to one another and to the community. The studies sought answers to such questions as: What are those congregations like? How did they get that way? More particularly, What style of pastoral and lay leadership has stimulated and developed those ministries?

Extended telephone interviews were conducted with 65 pastors. Thirty days were spent in 17 representative congregations, listening to pastors, staff, church officers, members, and people in the surrounding communities. Findings from interviews and congregational visits became the basis for a questionnaire on lay ministry which was completed by 98 pastors and 714 elders of these "ministering congregations." Their replies were compared statistically with replies to the same questionnaire from the Presbyterian Panel. This Panel consists of 3,800 United Presbyterians who have agreed to respond by mail to periodic attitude and opinion surveys on subjects of concern to the Agencies and Councils of the General Assembly. Participants are selected according to scientific sampling procedures so as to be representative of the opinions of United Presbyterian pastors, specialized ministers, elders, and members.

It is clear that these ministering congregations are different from most Presbyterian congregations. They range in size from under 50 members to more than 2,000 members. They are located in all parts of the nation; in the inner city, small towns, and suburbs. They are diverse in economic composition and in their theological perspectives. In spite of many differences, there are marked similarities in the pastoral and congregational styles among most of the congregations in the study. The common patterns that have been identified are set forth in the chapters that follow. Not all the congregations possess all the characteristics described here. However, most of them would recognize a striking similarity to themselves in these descriptions.

What Is Ministry?

Before analyzing the leadership styles of the ministering congregations we need to clarify what we mean by ministry.

Ministry is carrying out Christ's work in the world. In Jesus of Nazareth, the Creator of the universe became a human being. Although Jesus was the Messiah, the promised one of God, he became the Suffering Servant. He healed the sick, opened the eyes of the blind, and set captives free. Through his life, death, and resurrection, God reconciled the world to himself. So Jesus Christ is both our model for ministry and the source of energizing power which calls our ministries into being.

Ministry is the work of the church among its own members and in the world. It is carried out both corporately and individually and is not the exclusive responsibility of ordained ministers of the Word. In fact, it is the work of all the people of God.

God's call is to all people. From each of us it demands no less than total discipleship: to give our whole lives to God. Through baptism and confirmation every Christian affirms a positive response to God's call. We accept our vocation and are incorporated into the body of Christ. We become ministers in the world. We serve others on Christ's behalf.

It is not too much to say with Letty Russell, "Only as we see clearly that vocation and ministry are *not* options for *some* Christians, but are basic to the existence of *all* Christians, can we begin to make choices that might open up future and hope for the many needs of God's groaning and longing world."[1]

Many different functions are involved in ministry, and not every person will exercise all of these functions.

In our study, we deliberately chose a broad rather than a narrow definition of ministry to include the wide variety of concepts and patterns that exist in the church. Following the lead of James C. Fenhagen in *Mutual Ministry,*[2] we sought information about the activities of members in three areas:

1. *Ministries of caring.* Here we included ministries in times of crisis (illness, death, unemployment, divorce); ministries to special needs (the elderly, prisoners, the poor); and ministries through authentic community (fellowship, support, mutual caring, etc.).

2. *Ministries of justice and reconciliation.* Here we focused on the relationship of Christian values to decision-making in business, politics, and community; and the church members' involvement in issues such as hunger, racism, sexism; and the use or abuse of power in government and business.

3. *Ministries of witness and dialogue.* This involved sharing the gospel and one's Christian experience, and engaging in dialogue about the Christian faith and the meaning of life.

Ministry may be exercised corporately through programs of the congregation itself, or individually by the participation of particular Christians. Ministry may focus upon service to members of the congregation ("internal ministries") or upon service to people in the surrounding community ("external ministries").

Variations in the patterns of ministry within the congregations are too numerous to include in this study. However, examples will give concrete meaning to a broad concept of ministry as the work of God's people within the church and in the world.

How Congregations Engage in Ministry

The Covenant Church, in a small Midwestern community of 9,500, is noted throughout the county for its dedicated services to people in need. That congregation of 160 members has mobilized the resources of all the churches in the community to establish an ecumenical Agape Center which maintains an emergency food pantry and a clothing store. Donated garments are sold to people in need for a few cents apiece. The congregation brought a health fair to its community and has responded to emergency needs of people far beyond its own immediate area. The pastor likes to tell of an active deacon who was baptized as an adult just a few years ago. "Surely the Holy Spirit has got to be working in this man's life," she said as she told of the many ways he is continually serving other people. A few years ago there was a devastating flood in Pike-ville, Kentucky. Although this deacon had just arrived home from a trip, he rented a trailer and filled it with clothing that had been collected in the community. Within twenty-four hours he had driven 250 miles to the scene of the flood with immediate assistance for those who had lost everything.

Ministry in a Blighted Area

Old First Church, an integrated congregation of 280 members, is located in the midst of a heavily blighted area. Gutted old buildings remind one of the devastation of war. Members come from the immediate community and a wide surrounding area. All sorts of persons are attracted by the congregation's commitment to mission. An old home next to the church building provides hospitality to folks who walk in off the street. Referrals to community agencies, provision of financial aid, emergency food supplies, and counseling are all a part of the social service program directed by the congregation. A social worker, a street worker, and a community organizer assist the pastor and many lay volunteers.

There is a ministry of community organizing. The neighborhood association organized by Old First Church covers about six or seven blocks. It has been successful in getting better police response, in working on abandoned housing, and in fighting the sale of alcohol to minors. The pastor joined the head of a local mortgage company and the branch manager of the local bank in asking the Liquor Control Board to postpone the granting of a license to a pub that had been selling to minors and had been allowing vagrants to stand out in front of their store. The pastor's life was threatened, and various community leaders, including the mayor, called a press conference to declare their support of the movement. A twenty-four-hour prayer chain was organized among members of the congregation. A shot through a car window nearly hit one of the staff members of the congregation. Ministry in this context involves fighting for the life of the city, and for people who still live there.

A cross-cultural institute organized by the congregation is designed to promote understanding among the peoples of various cultures in the area. It works on discovering solutions to problems of racism and discrimination and educates leaders in building bridges between cultures of the neighborhood.

A "seminary of the community" provides vigorous lay theological education for adults who seek to understand their faith at greater depth. At the heart of all this dedicated flurry of advocacy and service is a warm, caring Christian community that worships and studies together.

Ministry in Suburbia

The Pleasant Lake Church, with over 2,000 members in an affluent suburban community, is alive with the excitement of ministry. Over fifty Koinonia groups, with 8 to 10 persons in each group, meet twice a month for sharing, study, and prayer. Members are ministering to one another and lives are being changed. Through a marriage encounter group a lawyer and his wife have come to a richer relationship in their marriage. His practice is heavily involved in divorce cases. His ministry has become a search for ways to help his clients save their marriages, even though this means a loss of potential legal fees.

Several members from the congregation have organized a Housing Opportunity Association. The church gave them $3,000 a year. Adding individual donations to this, they have secured enough money to make down payments on homes for families who have low credit ratings. They go to banks and arrange for mortgages in the name of the Association. When those who are buying the home pay off the down payment, the mortgage is transferred to their name.

Each member of the Association board establishes a personal counseling relationship with the new homeowners. From time to time this may involve them in such things as helping people get jobs, or food stamps, or financial assistance for paying heating bills. This highly successful program has now led to the ownership of seventeen homes and to sufficient income from debt repayments to buy two additional homes a year.

The congregation also has set aside $30,000 of its property as backing for a county bail fund. The people of the church started a youth program for predelinquent youngsters who have had one encounter with the law. This has now been taken over by the county.

Green Estates, a congregation of 435 members, is also located in an affluent suburb. The church budget provides generously for many community organizations in the metropolitan area. But the congregation will not provide funds for any project in which its members are not personally involved. Through a relationship with a neighborhood in the city, members supply food shelves, provide rape counseling, secure jobs, provide clothing, work with a child development center, assist in a school for the mentally retarded, and help in a halfway house for sex offenders.

Members of the congregation and others have organized a lobby in Washington for peace, and have helped presbytery develop a program that enables its congregations to deal with issues related to hunger. Out of a study of homosexuality grew joint action with neighboring congregations to work for human rights amendments in their metropolitan area. Thirty persons worked intensively for about six weeks to get their state legislature to pass a new gun control law.

The heart of the ministry of this widely recognized congregation has been the ministry to one another. This ministry takes place in the small group life of the congregation, and in its celebrations of worship and of intergenerational fellowship.

Ministry in a Changing Neighborhood

Grace Church is another affluent congregation located in an urban residential area of a large city. The neighborhood has been changing from 10 percent black ten years ago to 50 percent black today. The congregation, of perhaps 1,800 persons, comes from all over the city. When the neighborhood began to change, members who lived in the community began to move away. Then the session made a conscious choice—the church would stay. They would encourage members from all over the city to move into the neighborhood both to demonstrate the congregation's commitment to the area and to stabilize it as an interracial community. Their program includes a day-care center and a nursery school. Through an ecumenical consortium of churches they sponsor numerous community service activities and have organized an Urban Redevelopment Corporation that is helping to renew and beautify the neighborhood. The congregation has established a small youth industry program which employs young people of the community to make cassette tapes and crosses for sale all over the country. It is also working with a juvenile court judge in a low-income area to establish homes for juvenile delinquents who cannot return to their own homes.

If you drop in on a Friday evening, you will find the Grace Church buildings alive with people. Between 90 and 120 members of the Singles and Single Parents group are folk dancing and talking about their faith from their particular perspective. A majority of them are not members of the congregation. A College and Career group of perhaps a hundred young adults is engaged in Bible study.

The congregation has programs for senior citizens and a ministry to prisoners. A crisis counseling telephone ministry has led to the development of a drop-in counseling ministry. Members of the congregation are being trained for volunteer service as pastoral counselors. There are many different opportunities for adult education and Bible study. Many who are served by these and other programs attend worship services, and in turn are ministered to through a very active program of lay evangelism for which the congregation is noted.

Personal evangelism is the heart of this congregation's ministry. Every Tuesday evening, 45 to 50 members meet. In teams of two or three they call in the homes of persons who have attended the church or have requested a visit. One team member with experience serves as "presenter." Another may be a novice. They give their hosts a copy of the Good News New Testament and together read passages of Scripture. In a low-key, friendly way and without pressure, they seek a specific faith commitment to Jesus Christ where it does not already exist. They pray together. Team members are carefully trained to be sensitive to the person they are visiting and to respond to individual needs and concerns. Experienced team members are paired with those who are still developing their skills.

Ministry to Corporate Managers

One congregation has a significant number of members who are corporate officers of manufacturing companies with international business connections. Under the leadership of seminary faculty and denominational executives with overseas portfolios, a series of seminars have been held on such subjects as Christian ethics, liberation theology, human rights, and justice in developing nations. Through an active personal relationship with them, the pastor helps executives relate their faith to their responsibilities in business and their personal needs.

A Broad Range of Ministries

The ministering congregations in this study covered a broad range of perspectives and were involved in many different forms of ministry. Appendix 2 lists twenty different types of ministry most frequently engaged in. Over half of the 68 congregations that responded to those particular questions were engaged in the twenty types of ministry listed. Fourteen of the twenty types of ministry were focused more upon service to people in the community than upon service to members of the congregation.

The Congregation as Base for Ministry

Some advisers had urged that our study focus only on the ministry of the laity outside the life of the congregation. We decided, however, to include both ministries of church members to one another and their ministries in the community outside the congregation. This proved to be a fortunate choice in at least one respect. By looking at both "internal ministries" and "external ministries" at the same time we discovered that the two appear to be inextricably linked. Where a congregation or its members are actively involved in ministries outside the congregation, significant ministries to one anther always appear to be taking place within the fellowship of the congregation. When members of the congregation have personally experienced ministries of caring and have themselves learned to care for others within the fellowship of the people of God, they can then learn to care for and serve others outside that fellowship.

Of course, ministry to one another within the congregation does not automatically lead to ministries outside the congregation. Other leadership dimensions are required if that is to happen. One reason the church has had difficulty in developing lay ministry "in the world" may be that too frequently we have assumed that such ministries should be separated from ministries within the congregation. It is doubtful if that is possible.

Elizabeth O'Connor, of the Church of the Saviour in Washington, D.C., makes the same point in her book *Journey Inward, Journey Outward.* "We cannot begin to cope with what it means to build a world community unless we understand how difficult it is to be in community even with a small group of people, presumably called by their Lord to the same mission. Nor will we know the full power of the Spirit while we cling to our upper rooms. . . . We are going to know little about the task of reconciliation in the world unless we are in touch with what goes on in that world within ourselves and know how difficult reconciliation is there."[3]

Six Recurring Themes

The most striking discovery in our study of ministering congregations is that there are similarities among congregations that differ widely in theological emphasis, size, geographical location, and socioeconomic context.

The next seven chapters will elaborate on six major themes which recurred repeatedly. In summary they are:

Sounding a Clear Call (Chapter 2). Ministering congregations sound a clear call to the ministry of all the people. They have a clear vision of mission, are deeply committed to shared ministry, and celebrate together an exciting sense of identity. Pastors articulate the vision and motivate to action. Leaders are effective in communicating what is happening in the life of the congregation.

Discovering Grace as a Way of Life (Chapter 3). Members feel they are accepted as they are as well as for their potential. Leaders have high expectations for their service. Emphasis is placed on complete freedom to choose among many opportunities. Grace rather than guilt and legalism provides motivation. Pastors share their vulnerabilities along with their experiences of gospel resources.

Becoming a Caring Community (Chapter 4). Members feel that the congregation is a family that supports and cares for one another. This meets basic human needs in our current cultural context. But members also recognize that it is the Spirit that gives community and makes possible the unity that binds them together in their diversity. Worship nurtures the family of God. People learn to care because they have experienced caring. Preaching and teaching help channel their love to the world.

Renewal Through Relationships (Chapter 5). Renewal comes to ministering congregations through many opportunities for face-to-face interaction. A wide variety of small groups provide occasions for fellowship and study, and for the sharing of vulnerabilities, resources, and opportunities for service. Parish care programs use lay leadership to meet the pastoral needs of parishioners. Pastors and lay leaders are seen as models of caring concern.

Using the Gifts God Has Given (Chapter 6). Leaders believe that the Holy Spirit gives the church the gifts it needs. They are responsive to the needs, visions, and abilities of church members and to their initiative for service. They identify gifts, affirm them, cultivate them through small achievable steps of successful ministry, and match them with possibilities for ministry. Program is responsive to those gifts and to those initiatives.

Sharing Power as Partners (Chapter 7). Leaders in ministering congregations are committed to partnership in ministry. They struggle with themselves, and with others as necessary, to achieve true collegiality with each other and with all the people. They demonstrate forceful leadership. They structure the work of the congregation to ensure mutual ministry.

Coming Alive (Chapter 8). How change takes place. Some clues are given as to ways pastors and lay leaders may prepare themselves for more effective leadership. Suggestions are made for possible strategies which congregations may use if they wish to move toward more active partnership in ministry.

Serendipity: Membership Growth

One final observation. Nearly half of the ministering congregations indicated that they were growing in membership. Sixteen percent said that they had had a great increase in membership, and 32 percent indicated that there had been some increase in their membership over the last several years. Twenty-three percent of the congregations said there had been no change in membership in recent years. Since membership in the United Presbyterian Church as a whole has been decreasing since 1965, and there has been a 22 percent total loss in membership over the past ten years, these figures are significant. Furthermore, the criterion for selecting these congregations was not membership growth but participation of members in ministry to one another and in the community.

Undoubtedly, new members in ministering congregations

are involved in the work of the congregation in a relatively short time. Over one half of new members are involved within six months, and two out of three are involved within one year. Whether or not one can establish a relationship between active involvement in ministry and membership growth, both would appear to be related to church vitality.

CHAPTER 2

Sounding a Clear Call

<hr>

> If the trumpet-call is not clear, who will pre-
> pare for battle?
>
> (I Cor. 14:8, NEB)

There is no lack of clarity in the message of the ministering congregations. The trumpets are playing! The banners are flying! Pastors, officers, and members know who they are and where they are going. They are on the move together!

They have rediscovered what the church is meant to be, they are committed to a concept of ministry which involves all church members, and they have found their own unique mission and sense of identity.

I. WHAT THE CHURCH IS MEANT TO BE

The most important question any congregation can ask is, Who are we anyway? To some, the answer may seem so obvious that they fail to ask the question when they should. Familiar clichés do not go deep enough to awaken congregational vitality.

Perhaps the strongest thread that unites the ministering congregations to one another, in spite of their differences, is their theological understanding of the church as the people of God. Their calling is clear. It is to help the whole congregation discover what it means to be God's people in a particular time and place.

Rediscovering Our Roots

The Green Estates Church is noted for its active involvement in a wide range of social ministries. We have described some of them in Chapter 4. Over the years it has taken strong leadership in social action in the community and in the nation. A visitor is struck with the warmth, freedom, and rigor of its fellowship. "Behold, how they love one another," one is tempted to say.

The pastor tells of their pilgrimage:

> "About eight or nine years ago we began to ask the question what it meant to be a church in the twentieth century. As a congregation, we went back to the book of The Acts. We studied it for about six months, with one question in mind: 'What can the model tell us about the church now?' A real consensus began to emerge. One thing that was very impressive to us was that what drew people to that church was not a lot of doctrine or doubt but a desire to have a personal relationship with God. They had different ways of understanding it, and people were at different points with it. But what they had in common was that they wanted that relationship to grow."

Out of their study of The Acts, the Green Estates congregation committed themselves to three things: study, sharing, and serving. Through study they sought to understand the good news and the apostles' teachings. Through sharing each other's burdens and joys they discovered what it means to be "members one of another." They committed themselves to share financially and sought to become "a radical 10 percent community." Their goal has been for every member to be a tither. Serving became their enthusiastic avenue of reaching out beyond themselves in a ministry to the world.

Renewed as a Servant People

Historic John Knox Church in downtown Capitol City was planning its two hundredth anniversary. Instead of turning to their past, the people chose as their theme "Renewed as a Servant People."

For some time the pastor and a group of lay leaders had been exploring in depth the meaning of the church and its mission in the world. Two hundred members of the congregation joined in the enterprise by reading two books, *Agents of Reconciliation* by Arnold Come and *Christ and Culture* by Richard Niebuhr. The congregation spun off into task groups that examined every phase of the church's life in the light of their theme. Out of grappling with the deepest meanings of the church and its mission in the world came a vision of what their church might be. That vision has ignited the imaginations of pastor and members and has led them into an exciting period of renewed vitality, to ecumenical partnership with neighboring congregations, and to active service in their community.

Like these two churches, other ministering congregations have experienced renewed vitality through a rediscovery of the roots of the Christian church. There is no one way in which a congregation may come to a clear image of what the church is meant to be. One thing is axiomatic, however. No matter how it is achieved, clarity regarding the nature of the church and commitment to its mission is absolutely essential. Without it, a ministering congregation is an impossibility.

Biblical Images of the Church

Ministering congregations are united in their understanding of the church as the people of God. Their pastors readily articulate that understanding of ministry based upon deep Biblical and theological convictions. They affirm that ministry is the work of all church members, not just the task of the pastor and the staff.

A congregation seeking to unlock latent resources for ministry lying dormant in its membership may do well to study some of the Biblical images of the church. These images affirm the crucial importance of *all* the people of God as servants of God's purposes in the world. This can be illustrated by a quick look at some of those images.

1. The People of God (*laos theou*)

Thomas W. Gillespie in his illuminating exposition of "The Laity in Biblical Perspective" points out that the Greek word *laos* was used in the Septuagint for the Hebrew word '*am*. This in turn is used almost exclusively for Israel—the chosen people of God.

In this close association with Israel, laos loses its general meaning of "crowd" or "population," and takes on the sense of a specific people, a people not in "mass," but in "union" because of the unique call of God.[4]

Today we also are called to be the people of God—to carry out God's mission in the world. All Christians are part of the *laos.* All believers, without exception, are sent into the world as witnesses and servants.

Unfortunately, in our time the word "laity" has lost the powerful symbolism of the word *laos,* from which it is derived. In common usage we contrast "laity" with "clergy" or with "professional." Laity are usually perceived as "less than clergy" or as "not as well qualified as professionals." Clearly, it is of fundamental importance that we recapture the positive idea that ministry is the work of all the people of God.

2. The Body of Christ

The figure of the body of Christ and its many parts (Eph. 4 and I Cor. 12) places forceful emphasis on the importance to the body of even its most insignificant member. Each interdependent part possesses gifts which serve the other interdependent parts. The parts are whole only as they are actively engaged in serving one another. In other words, ministry is an inherent function of bodily maintenance and growth. Furthermore, it seems clear that any healthy body exists for more than its own maintenance. The internal ministry of one part of the body to another is in order to enable the body itself to minister to the whole of creation.

3. A Servant People

When our Lord gave to all of us the institution of the Last Supper, he did so within the context of washing the disciples' feet. As Suffering Servant Messiah he still comes to us and says, "If I, your Lord and Master, have washed your feet, you also ought to wash one another's feet." All Christians are called to be servants to one another and to the world just as their Lord was servant to them. Again, the church consists of *all* God's people and they are *all* servants, or ministers.

4. Ministers of Reconciliation

We live in a world of alienation. Forces of contemporary life reinforce our human condition of estrangement from one another, from ourselves, and from God. This makes the message of our reconciliation in Jesus Christ of increasing urgency and promise. In Christ we are new creatures.

All this is from God, who through Christ reconciled us to himself and gave us the ministry of reconciliation. (II Cor. 5:18)

Our calling as the church of Jesus Christ is to be ministers of reconciliation. This goes beyond service. Arnold Come, in his book *Agents of Reconciliation,* points out that the translation of *diakonia* as "ministry" rather than as "service" gives fresh meaning to our calling. A servant obeys the master but does not share in the master's life and purposes. " 'Service' becomes 'ministry' when the Someone and the Something served become immanent in the life of the servant, when the life and cause of the Served become the life and cause of the servant —joyfully, actively, voluntarily."[5]

5. Royal Priesthood

In his Biblical study of the laity, Gillespie relates the call of the people of God to service as a royal priesthood. He quotes I Peter 2:9–10:

But you are a chosen race, a royal priesthood, a holy nation, God's own people, that you may declare the wonderful deeds of him who called you out of darkness into his marvelous light. Once you were no people but now you are God's people; once you had not received mercy but now you have received mercy.

Just as Israel was called to serve as "a kingdom of peace and a holy nation in behalf of the kingdoms and nations of the world," so also are the whole people of God to serve a contemporary priestly function. All of us together are to play a mediating ministry for Jesus Christ in behalf of the world. Our priesthood is not only our own direct access to God; it is also the service we render on behalf of others.

Gillespie concludes that whenever the church has fallen into the trap of identifying the work of the clergy as *"the* ministry," the result is a "theological disaster." When that happens, the laity abandon their ministries. Leaving the principal role of ministry to the "clergy," they relegate themselves to the role of a supporting cast.

6. A Living Temple

Again, Gillespie describes the Biblical image of God's people as a living temple:

God's "dwelling" upon earth is a people rather than a building, a Holy people "set apart" for God rather than from the world, a people mandated to mission rather than coddled in seclusion, a people called by God to the living of salvation in the matrix of everyday life rather than delivered from life's cares and responsibilities, a people who live "before God" at all times and in all places rather than lead double lives in segregated sacred and secular compartments. Ministry in such a temple-community can only be worldward in its thrust.[6]

The Pastor's Equipping Ministry

These six Biblical images, and many more, set forth the clear and consistent Biblical warrant for the calling of all believers to ministry. What, then, is the role of the minister of the Word? Perhaps that question, more than any other, carries the greatest threat to the professional minister who seeks to implement the concept of the ministry of the laity. If we take seriously the ministry which belongs to every church member, does that imply a less meaningful task for ministers of the Word?

On the contrary, the task of ordained ministers is even more challenging. No longer is it necessary for the pastor to shoulder the burden of personally carrying out all the tasks of ministry. Rather, the pastor's calling is to prepare and sustain members of the body as they exercise their ministries to one another and in the community. It is to equip the saints for their ministries. Or, more accurately, it is to provide the stimulus and the leadership which the people need to equip one another for their common ministries. Pastors of ministering congregations have discovered that this exciting, fulfilling, and liberating challenge more than makes use of all their gifts.

Various Bible passages speak of a diversity of gifts given to the church. In Ephesians we read:

And his gifts were that some should be apostles, some prophets, some evangelists, some pastors and teachers, to equip the saints for the work of ministry, for building up the body of Christ. (Eph. 4:11–12)

In his work *The Theology of the Laity,* Hendrik Kraemer[7] points out that the Greek text does not support putting a comma after the phrase "to equip the saints." This change in the customary way of reading this passage underscores the ministry of the whole people of God, and also gives a sharp focus to the calling of the pastoral ministry.

What United Presbyterians Believe About Ministry

The official description of ministry for the United Presbyterian Church is clearly set forth in the *Book of Order.*

All believers participate in the ministry of Jesus Christ who is at once God's word of revelation and work of reconciliation. This ministry is Jesus' ministry by word and deed through the Holy Spirit. Christ is the minister and servant of God in whom and through whom the whole Church and every member of the Church is called to ministry. It is expected of all that they shall serve God through his Church, both to the building of its inner life and to the extension of its service to the world, to the end that every knee shall bow and every tongue confess that Jesus Christ is Lord.

Within this ministry there are some who are called by Christ and set apart by ordination, to perform special tasks in the life of the Church. Although no absolute distinction may be drawn between these and other Christians, since there are diversities of gifts but the same Spirit, a distinction of office is acknowledged; and certain tasks in the life of the Church are reserved for those ordained to fulfill them. Those ordained to the ministry of Word and sacraments have entrusted to them the direction and leading of public worship, with special responsibility for the proclamation of the Word of God in preaching and in the administration of the sacraments. (*Book of Order,* Directory for the Worship of God, Ch. I, Sec. 4)

A series of different but overlapping statements about the meaning of ministry were submitted to the Presbyterian Panel as well as to elders and pastors of the ministering congregations.

Members and elders of the United Presbyterian Church are somewhat ambivalent about the meaning of ministry. On the one hand, three fourths of them agree that ministry is the special work of the pastor which serves the spiritual needs of the congregation. On the other hand, they recognize that the way they live out their faith in relation to family, friends, neighborhood, and occupation is also ministry. And they affirm the idea of the ministry of the laity in their own lives. Surprisingly, almost two thirds of the members and three fourths of the elders in the Panel said they think of themselves as ministers to the people around them either "daily" or "weekly."

United Presbyterian ministers as represented in the Panel have opinions about ministry that are considerably different from those of most members and elders. Only 40 percent of them agree with their parishioners that ministry is the special work of the pastor. And they are much more likely than members and elders in the Panel to affirm that ministry includes corporate action by the church to change unjust economic or political conditions.

Pastors agree more strongly than elders and members that ministry includes the way a member lives out his or her faith in relation to family, friends, neighborhood, and occupation. They are also more likely to say that ministry is the shared work of the whole congregation which serves the people of the congregation.

It is clear that there is strong theological support among United Presbyterian ordained ministers for the concept of lay ministry.

How Ministering Congregations Differ

Pastors of ministering congregations differ significantly from other Presbyterian pastors in their definitions of ministry at one point. Along with elders in their churches, they are more likely to agree that ministry includes corporate action by the church to change the unjust economic or political conditions of life.

Elders in ministering congregations are less likely than elders in the Panel to agree that ministry is the special work of the pastor. Also they agree more readily than Panel elders that ministry includes the ways a member lives out his or her faith in relation to family, friends, and neighborhood. In this they do not differ significantly from their own pastors in ministering congregations. In other words, the idea of the ministry of the whole people of God is much more vital to elders in the ministering congregations than it is among elders in the United Presbyterian Church as a whole. These elders have stronger convictions about partnership in ministry and hold a broader, more inclusive, concept of ministry.

Whereas there still are significant differences between elders and pastors of the ministering congregations in their understanding of ministry, on the whole those understandings are more nearly congruent with one another than is the case in other United Presbyterian congregations represented by the Panel.

II. COMMITMENT TO PARTNERSHIP IN MINISTRY

Pastors of ministering congregations differ with other pastors, not so much in what they *say* about the ministry of the whole people of God but in what they do about it.

They are deeply committed to partnership in ministry. The ministry of the laity is not simply icing on the cake, it is the meat and potatoes and the cake itself. Therefore, shared ministry has become the singular focus of their lifework. They study it, think about it, teach it, preach it, talk with individuals about it, and have learned the specific skills to practice it.

Comments from two pastors are typical:

"Shared ministry is my fundamental stance. I communicate with the session and with the board of deacons and with the congregation very clearly. This is not my ministry. This is our ministry. And that includes their ministry to one another as well as their ministry within the community."

"We have devoted our energies over the past twenty years, not to being the ones who do the work of the church, but to being the ones who see that the work of the church is done. That has established a tremendous sense of partnership in our congregation. We all resource and support each other. We bring our particular training and gifts and skills to bear upon the life of the church as we journey along. We genuinely believe as professionals and lay people alike that we all have something to bring."

A Long Tradition

A number of the ministering congregations have had a long tradition of partnership in ministry. Partnership in ministry does not come to full flower overnight. Many years of patient tending of the tender plant often precedes fruition. Several of the congregations have had a succession of pastors who have emphasized the ministry of all church members. And in some cases the current pastor was called because of his or her commitment to shared ministry. Two other pastors make that clear in what they say about their congregations.

"There is a pretty broad assumption here that has been built over the years and prior to my ministry. Christians are called to ministry as a part of the faith community. The faith community belongs to them. And they have a ministry out in the larger community and in the world."

"People here have been trained for many years . . . to think of their life in the church as preparation for their ministry in the world. The pastor who preceded me had a strong sense that the church was to be an equipping center: its primary task was to enable people to be effective in the world and to represent Christ there. He preached it. He taught it. And I was surprised to find the level of understanding and living out of that principle when I came."

Articulating the Vision

"He preached it. He taught it." Those words could be re-peated over and over again. Pastors of ministering congrega-tions persistently articulate the vision of the ministry of all the people. Challenges to involvement are given consistently, re-peatedly, publicly, privately, and individually, in general terms and in specific terms. One is aware of this as one listens to the preaching and participates in worship. Members of the congregation affirm it in many ways:

> "The entire program of the church last fall was oriented toward our ministries: what they are and the opportunities that there are for ministry. Ministry is not something that you go and do, but something you do as you go."

> "In our liturgy there are sections labeled 'pastor' and 'ministers.' When we respond as ministers I say to myself, 'Hey, what am I going to do about that?' "

Pastors of ministering congregations are much more likely than other pastors to communicate the importance and pos-sibilities of ministry by church members, and to motivate members to be involved in service in the community. Elders recognize that emphasis in their pastor's ministry.

Making Real the Needs for Ministry

Another high priority for pastors of ministering congrega-tions is the focusing of attention on issues outside the congrega-tion and the interpreting of them from Biblical and theological perspectives. Again, this is in marked contrast to the priorities of pastors of other congregations. Under the leadership of the pastors in ministering congregations, members become aware of crucial issues in the community, the nation, or the world. They are challenged to involve themselves in community ser-vice.

> "Our pastor," says one elder, "is concerned about what is hap-pening to his members and to the world around us. They are one. As you listen to him you feel he is taking you beyond the

Sunday morning sermon. When you hear the challenge to ministry from a person in whom you have confidence, you respond."

The session of Old First Church was telling about their involvement in ministry. One of the elders said: "I don't know when Reverend Jones is going to get combat pay, but I think he should. Whenever you try to solve a problem, you become part of that problem. We didn't have any abandoned houses until Reverend Jones came, you know. We didn't have muggings until he came. We didn't have any rats or roaches, or any fire hazards. When he came, fire hazards started and roaches began. The gangs were forming. As soon as we began to work with the youth, the people in the community said we didn't have these thugs around here before. Because we were trying to minister to the people we got involved and we became a part of that problem."

Pastors and sessions in ministering congregations find many different ways to remind people of specific needs that can be met through the ministries of the congregation.

The community surrounding the Saint James Church was experiencing a rapid influx of Spanish-speaking people. To help members of the congregation get more deeply involved in the community, the session established a Human Resources Task Force. Its task was to encourage the use of the congregation's human resources in the community. The task force identified community programs and agencies in need of volunteer service, and publicized the programs and the opportunities. This was a major focus of the congregation for several years. When asked what encouraged the high level of ministry in the Saint James congregation one of its members said: "They get you in a corner and show you a need. Then, when they are enthusiastic about service which will meet that need, somehow you get enthusiastic, too."

Signing on the Dotted Line

A need for service, in itself, is not enough to get people involved in ministry. Awareness of need must lead to commitment of resources. Time, energy, skill, imagination, and money are all involved in meeting those needs. Ministering congregations are more likely than other congregations to challenge their members in specific ways to participate in community activities. They get people to sign on the dotted line.

In the early years the Green Estates Church was forming new patterns of congregational life. The pastor would preach about specific opportunities for community service, and challenge members to commit themselves to undertake specific ministries. He actually would stand at the door of the church with a clipboard in his hands as the people were leaving the Sunday morning service, asking persons one by one to "sign up." Members of the congregation suggest that such pressure might not be effective today. But those early memories are part of a tradition which now expects everyone to get involved in specific ministries.

One of the current elders of the Green Estates Church tells of how he was first attracted to that congregation. In a personal conversation the pastor set before him the challenge of a particular opportunity. He asked a question that has remained with that elder over the years: "What are you doing that is more important than doing more for others?"

III. A Clear Vision of a Unique Mission

Beyond understanding the mission of the church, and an active commitment to the ministry of the whole people of God, ministering congregations are on the march because they have a clear sense of purpose and direction. They are not trying to be all things to all people. They know who they are and what they stand for. The emphasis in one congregation will differ significantly from the emphasis in another. Whatever it is, the banners are flying! The trumpets are playing! The people are on the march together! A common vision draws them forward.

Whatever the major emphasis, a particular ministering congregation always has a clear and consistent sense of direction, a strong sense of purpose, and a contagious feeling of identity.

Ministering congregations do differ significantly in their theological orientation and in what they understand their mission
to be. But they all have a vision, and a strong orientation
toward fulfilling that mission. Their pastors seem to be forceful
preachers and effective teachers, providing the members with
a clear rationale for the mission of the congregation and the
ministries of its people.

These churches compromise neither their vision nor their
message in encouraging others to join them. They welcome
those who wish to go where they are going, and they do not
reject those who are not on that road. There are other
churches to which those can go who do not share in the vision.

The pastor of the Green Estates Church put it this way: "We
think it is important that the church not be an echo, but give
people an opportunity to choose between ways of carrying out
their faith. And so we have said who we are and what we
expect. I think people like that. You know, you can't just play
to the median all the time and expect to have any quality."

Mary Jones describes her six-year ministry as pastor of the
Covenant Church in a small Midwestern community:

"I give the work of the Holy Spirit full credit. When I came here,
this was a dying congregation. The people were hungry for
spiritual feeding and to be challenged. Before coming, I had
made it known that if the people don't want to go strongly into
mission, they don't want me. In order to survive, this church had
to have an identity. We will never be able to compete with the
gorgeous, beautiful, physical plants of the other churches around
town. But we can compete and surpass in Christian love and
outreach. That is what this church has become well known for.

"Every church needs a unique personality. The Covenant
Church is known as 'the mission church—people who want to
get involved.' This attracts that kind of person. As one member
said to an inquiring friend, 'If you are not intersted in being
involved, you won't fit into that church.'

"I expect God to do something. Then I get out and help it to
happen. There is no such thing as a small church. There is nothing you can't do if you believe in it. When you have vision,

people dare to dream the impossible. I believe in trying to get the whole church involved. I am especially drawn to the 'grungies' of society. There is nothing more exciting in ministry than to get people to believe in themselves."

As one talks with this "woman of the Lord," feels her enthusiasm, and glimpses her vision, it is not difficult to understand why the Covenant congregation is alive with ministry.

Articulating the Dream

Forty-three percent of the pastors of ministering congregations say they give very high priority to clearly articulating a dream for the congregation. Thirty-seven percent of the elders in those congregations agree. In contrast, only 24 percent of the pastors in the Panel and 23 percent of the elders in the Panel believe their pastor gives very high priority to this function. Similarly, a much higher percentage of both pastors and elders in the ministering congregations than in the Panel believe that the members of their congregation have a clear sense of the congregation's purpose.

The goal orientation of ministering congregations is clearly one of their important characteristics.

In some cases this "dream" is seen as coming from the vision of the pastor. Members of the Green Estates Church say of their organizing pastor: "He had a dream that was big enough to capture people's imagination. He was charismatic, directive, and magnetic in his style."

More often, however, the dream has evolved through the interaction of pastor and members. It may be worked out through an extensive process of study and reflection. Often it tends to be formulated in a few words which become symbols of what the church stands for.

One congregation will speak of itself as an equipping center. Its task is to equip members for ministry to one another and for involvement in Christ's work in the world. The members also feel called to equip leaders from other congregations who come to share the vision with them.

Another congregation speaks of three foci for its work: *recruitment* (encouraging people to become disciples, or followers, of Christ), *renewal* (nurturing God's people), and *reaching out* (acting in society).

A third congregation says that its motto is "To know Christ, to serve him, and to make him known."

The dream may take different forms. It may be a strong thrust in personal evangelism. It may be active involvement in community service. It may be a witness to the community through involvement in social action.

Saint John's Church, located in a blue-collar residential community, involved its session and members in a study of their mission. At the conclusion of their study they decided to emphasize corporate involvement in ministry rather than individual involvement. The congregation as a body has developed its ministries to and in the community. It has urged the members to participate in the community ministries carried on by the congregation rather than to work individually through various community organizations.

In contrast to this, many of the ministering congregations in upper-middle-class suburban communities tend to encourage their members, as individuals, to become involved in community agencies.

Old First Church, in the heart of a decayed inner-city neighborhood, finds that the pressure of human need is very great. The temptation to paternalism is equally great. To avoid that temptation, the session of Old First Church has defined its particular community of faith as the whole urban community within which the congregation is serving. Under the influence of an ordained woman staff member from Europe, the church has learned to speak of "mission in reverse," and say, "We are not here to help the least of these brethren. But we are all here to work with each other. Consequently we feel that the community is our teacher. Very often people whom we serve also serve us in reverse. For example, we might provide transportation for a family to get to the hospital, or to get to the grocery store. But they in turn might provide housing or hospitality for somebody who comes to visit us, for someone who comes to see what we are about. People in the community minister to the congregation just as the congregation ministers to the community."

A Strong Sense of Identity

These illustrations underscore the strong sense of identity which characterizes the ministering congregations. That sense of identity has compelling power to attract and unite people in spite of their differences. It may be expressed through deep-rooted traditions or through symbolic language and symbolic acts.

The Forest Canyon Church sees itself as a congregation that attracts creative and rather sophisticated persons who are disillusioned with traditional religious expression. Members feel their pastor is able to formulate the Christian faith in contemporary terms. They value the freedom which they enjoy. They are freed through fresh approaches to their religious experience.

Members of the Forest Canyon Church believe that their creativity is released through widespread participation in seasonal festivals which involve the whole congregation in celebration. They see themselves as catalysts in the lives of individuals and in the corporate life of the community. They believe that their lives, their religion, their faith, and the world are all intertwined. They affirm a "theology of involvement" which leads to personal growth but which also recognizes that such growth is intimately related to involvement with the rest of the community.

The Green Estates Church expresses its identity through a series of sharply focused image words and phrases. Its members have mastered the use of symbolic words and symbolic acts. We have already spoken of their commitment of study, sharing, and serving. Other phrases capture some of their traditions as a congregation. The phrases "The Green Estates Experience" and "In typical Green Estates fashion" are used to reinforce experiences that members feel are particularly expressive of their family style or of their openness to change.

A number of the Green Estates watchwords express their belief in the value of change. They speak of "continuing to grow" or of the "journey" on which they are embarked. They can be heard to say, "I can learn something new." They see themselves as dynamic and responsive to change. "Will things ever be the same around here again?" the pastor asked in a sermon. Replying to his own question, he asked again, "Are they ever the same around here?" There is great variety in their worship experiences to which they are apt to say with a chuckle, "This is not a normal Sunday."

Members of the Green Estates congregation give financial priority to community service and community action, not to bricks and mortar. They reinforce this commitment by referring to the architecture of their place of worship as "Early Gymnasium," or by talking about "the driveway" or "the unpaved parking lot." They joke about finding themselves "knee-deep in mud" whenever it rains.

Just as they have symbolic words and phrases, so also the members of the Green Estates congregation share symbolic acts. They hug one another, hold hands, dress casually, worship "in the round," and share their joys and concerns in informal ways during the Sunday morning worship celebration.

The Impact of Identity

It is clear that there are many ways in which a strong sense of identity enhances the life and work of the congregation. It attracts like-minded people who share a common vision. The church gets a reputation. Symbolic words and acts communicate what the congregation values. People in the community, or even in a wide surrounding area, understand what the congregation stands for. If they agree with its goals, if its emphases meet particular needs, or if they are seeking opportunities to render a particular kind of service, they come, and soon become a part of the fellowship.

If a man is seeking a stronger evangelistic emphasis and a congregation is noted for such an emphasis, he will be attracted to that congregation. If a woman feels that her congregation has badly neglected its responsibility for social service or social action, she will seek the fellowship of those who give priority to ministry in the community.

The Foothill Church has doubled its membership in the last five years. It is noted for its fellowship and for the way in which its members involve themselves in its life and work.

It is a Sunday evening in the Foothill Church. A small group of young adults are gathered in one of the homes for Bible study with the pastor. They have been sharing why it is that they are involved in ministry to one another. A guest has been listening intently. She begins to speak.

"I was always a Christian. When I was nineteen I got married. My husband had no use for the church. So I drifted away from it. Now I'm twenty-seven. My marriage has broken up and I realize how much I have been missing. I have come back to Christ. As you know, I work for Joseph Brown. Not long ago he told me I should go over to the Foothill Church, so I did.

"The first Sunday, in the fellowship hour following the service Joanne came over and dumped on me. She unloaded all her problems. I found I was ministering to her. Then the other day my boss asked, 'How's it going?' 'Not so good,' I told him. 'The problem is fellowship,' he said. 'Go back to Foothill. Go to Bill Stevens' Bible study.' So here I am! I'm an activist—and you say you are involved. You say you have to extend yourself—to learn and to grow. That's the kind of person I am. You talk about fellowship. That's what I want. I guess you've got me. I won't promise, but I'll probably be back."

And so another potential member has found her way into the fellowship—by the reputation of a congregation that seems to meet her specific needs.

In small towns and naturally homogeneous rural communities, a clear identity for the congregation can play an important part in giving meaning and drive to the ministries of the people of God.

A strong sense of identity generates contagious enthusiasm among the members of a congregation and communicates a climate of vitality. People feel very good about their congregation and tell others how they feel. Commitment of people to the church is deepened. To use an old cliché, "Nothing succeeds like success."

Members of ministering congregations often feel that their particular congregation is unique. There could not possibly be another congregation like them. They have a sense of pride in who they are.

There is an almost messianic quality about these congregations. Their proud feelings of identity are readily translated into a sense of mission—to help other congregations and to find what is so precious to them. "Because we are unique," some will say, "we have something important to contribute to other churches."

But pride can also be a liability. In more than one of the ministering congregations there is a keen awareness of the dangers of spiritual pride and potential exclusion. Comments go something like this:

> "Maybe we feel too good about ourselves. I think sometimes we tend to be elitist. We get to feeling that we're ahead of everybody else, and that bothers me a little bit. When we think of sliding back, we are comparing ourselves to what other less desirable churches are like. Some who move away to other communities feel that there is nothing like our congregation, so they drop out altogether."

As one reflects on the vitality of the ministering congregations, one is struck with the maturity of their self-understanding.

They have caught a vision of what the church is meant to be and are seeking to be faithful to that vision. They have joined hands in common commitment to partnership in ministry and are seeking to discover how shared ministry can become a reality. They have responded to a unique calling and to a particular pattern of ministry that has captured their imaginations and has given them a sense of fulfillment and achievement. They exhibit a remarkable blend of pride and humility. Somehow they are able to combine a clear focus of mission with a capacity to accept those who differ from them. They have purpose without exclusivism. Those who come into their fellowship are free to be themselves. Yet they are being led forward into the possibility of becoming more than they ever dared dream they could be. In being called into the fellowship of believers they have been blessed with a vital contemporary experience of the meaning of grace. They are the church of Jesus Christ!

CHAPTER 3

Discovering Grace as a Way of Life

> We can only love because we are born out of
> love, . . . we can only give because our life is
> a gift, . . . we can only make others free be-
> cause we are set free by Him whose heart is
> greater than ours. . . . We can be free to let
> others enter into the space created for them
> and allow them to dance their own dance,
> sing their own song and speak their own lan-
> guage without fear.
> (Henri Nouwen, *The Wounded Healer*)[8]

Ministering congregations have discovered the exciting possibilities of grace as a way of life. Their members frequently
say: "We are involved in ministry because we are loved and
accepted as we are. We do not need to pretend to be something more than that. There is no one who is going to condemn
us." Because they are accepted, they can accept themselves—
and others.

The Power of Grace

God's grace makes all things new. In Jesus Christ, God accepts us as we are. Having experienced that acceptance, we
can accept ourselves as we are. We can unmask ourselves and
admit that we are less than we would like to be. We then
recognize shortcomings and failures as part of our human condition and discover the joy of forgiveness and fellowship with
God.

Because we learn to accept ourselves, we can accept others too. They also have human failings, as we do. They also are accepted, as we are. Through grace we discover the deep meaning of our common humanity. Since neither of us has deserved the love of God, we share a common life in Christ. Each of us has been forgiven so much that whatever we must forgive in one another is really nothing at all. As with the ungrateful servant in Jesus' parable (Matt. 18:23–35), our canceled debt runs into millions of dollars, while our fellow servant may owe us a few paltry dollars. God's unconditional love calls us to love and serve others.

One congregation may put this in very traditional terminology. People speak of personal commitment to Jesus Christ and of being saved by grace through faith. They tell us that they are willing to say yes to ministry because of the gratitude they feel for all that Christ has done for them. Their experience of grace makes them want to respond. They serve because they want to, not out of a sense of obligation.

Accepting Your Acceptance

Another congregation may avoid familiar religious terminology. They speak more readily of acceptance than of grace. Members have been attracted to their congregation because of its freshness of approach and because of its openness to different points of view. They welcome the dialogue that comes when they feel their doubts are openly dealt with and when different perspectives are encouraged. They are grateful for the freedom they have discovered, because their congregation "celebrates humanity" rather than condemning it. They talk of salvation as wholeness, and rejoice that "people become alive again and want to work."

As a member of the Forest Canyon Church put it:

"Our pastor basically encourages people to be themselves and not be straightjacketed into the religious ritualistic beliefs that most of us were brought up with as kids. These have basically pushed me farther and farther away from being interested in the church. He encourages people to be themselves. Repeatedly during his first year with us he said: 'You are accepted. Accept your acceptance.' You don't have to conform to someone else's belief. What you believe is all right."

Their acceptance has renewed them, and made them want to serve others.

Acceptance in some congregations clearly means the freedom to be one's self in terms of dress or manner or life-style. "People are attracted to our congregation because they feel that anything is acceptable. There is an evident support and an informal atmosphere and a warmth to which they respond."

Acceptance of Diversity

In many congregations acceptance of diversity is part of a ministry of inclusiveness.

"People get the impression that this is definitely an open congregation. It is not closed by any means. It is open to all people and to all races and colors.

"The desire to be involved comes out of an openness, of an inclusiveness. I think it is a liberal church with a conservative theology. Liberal in the sense of our life-style."

The pastor of the John Knox Church likes to speak of a "network of grace" in which there is a mutual acceptance by people of one another. People get help and people give help. He preaches a ministry of inclusiveness, and members of the congregation have learned to be accepting, responsive, and caring of the widely diverse people who come in from the neighborhood to worship and share in their life. They have learned to believe that the gospel is for all, including people on drugs, unmarried persons living together, homosexuals, and others who may differ widely from them.

Grace at work in the ministering congregations is not passive acceptance. It is active, nonjudgmental, love that cares for the person at whatever point that person may be. It is the kind of love seen in the father running to throw his arms around the prodigal. It is the woman who searches for the lost coin or the shepherd who seeks the one lost sheep.

In a world of alienation, separation, and loneliness people discover that Christian fellowship is a haven of caring and accepting love. Whatever their background or circumstances, persons count for something.

How is it, for example, that the Green Estates Church has a large number of single parents and divorced persons in the congregation? A group of its members were discussing that question. They told of the importance of an accepting and caring community. In other congregations in which they had been members, such people would have felt out of place or unwelcome. In Green Estates, on the other hand, not only do the people feel that they are accepted, they are actually drawn closer to the caring community. The love of the community reaches out in a troubled time and offers support. Not only do members who divorce not leave Green Estates, but others who have been divorced are attracted to it.

How does a congregation come to be open and accepting to all sorts of people? Usually it is through people who are the personification of grace in action. It is through people who accept others where they are; whose attitude is: "I'll love them whatever they do. I'm a sinner too. Nothing will shock me."

The Foothill Church is in a comfortable racially intergrated residential neighborhood in a large metropolitan area. It has been going through a period of redevelopment. The people have come alive to the possibilities of ministering to one another and in the community. The pastor of the Foothill Church is perceived as accepting, nonjudgmental, and helpful. He "deals with people wherever they happen to be." As one member put it:

> "I think I know why I came to Foothill. It is because of the unusual nonverbal and persuasive ministry of our pastor. He reached out to me because I was lost. He was concerned about me, but willing to let me take my own time. He listened to me, but wouldn't give me answers. He gave me books to read. I realized that if I really wanted to learn, I would have to be a part of that church. The next thing I knew I was 'hooked.'"

The Pleasant Lake Church had been a successful downtown pulpit-oriented congregation. They relocated in the suburbs and a new pastor came with a vision of involving all the people in ministry. That was many years ago and another pastor has succeeded him. Looking back on their history, a group of the leaders reflected on the transforming impact of accepting love in the life of that pastor.

> "It was a personal kind of ministry. He made people feel loved and important and it came through in every single thing he did. He was really like that, whether he was speaking from the pulpit or speaking to you personally. I remember when we went to see a young girl in the hospital. There had been a tragedy in the family. Speaking of our pastor, she said to me, 'Just to shake his hand as I come out of church makes me feel as if I am really important and really loved.' "

Not Our Past, but Our Potentials

Grace at work in the ministering congregations leads beyond acceptance of people where they are. It deals with them in terms of their potential. One pastor wrote in a communication to his parish: "What made Jesus so attractive to those who knew him was his willingness to see them for their possibilities rather than their past. What he did was to hold before them a vision of what they might become, rather than a picture of what they had been."

Thus members feel the inner calling to growth and to service. They feel validated. They are needed. They count as persons. They can make a difference. Because they are loved and accepted, they have been given the freedom to love and accept others. Grace opens the door to growth.

One session member said of her pastor, "His openness, his sharing of himself, his love of people, accepts them where they are but leaves them with a desire to be more than they are."

Free to Take Risks

Acceptance also frees people to take risks. Because they are accepted, they can afford to fail, for failure will not lead to rejection. Grace allows people to make their own mistakes. It gives them the right to fail. Love will be waiting for them regardless of the outcome. "It's okay to fail," people will say. And so it is less threatening to try something new.

Risk-taking has been central to the life of the Forest Canyon Church. One of their leaders attributes this directly to the concept of grace.

> "Over and over again we have heard: 'You are accepted. Accept your acceptance.' It's really okay to go all out in whatever it is that you are doing, because things won't come tumbling down on you if it doesn't work out right. Or if something doesn't conform, you won't have some sort of guilt trip laid on you because you did it wrong. You are accepted and that's okay."

Confidence and Self-Worth

Through a firsthand experience of grace, members of ministering congregations develop confidence and feelings of self-worth. Parishioners will say, "He helped me to see a lot in myself . . . to recognize my potential and feel good about myself." Or a pastor will say, "I want to help them discover the wonderful people they were meant to be."

In fact, one significant difference between pastors of ministering congregations and those in the Presbyterian Panel is in this area. Fifty-six percent of the pastors of ministering congregations say that they give high priority to developing confidence and feelings of self-worth in church members. Forty-four percent of the elders in their congregations agree that this is the case. For pastors and elders in the Panel the figures are 40 percent and 27 percent.

High Expectations

Most ministering congregations warmly welcome into their fellowship all those who wish to share in that fellowship. They do, however, expect those who become members to take their membership seriously. This is part of accepting people for their potential. Leaders in these congregations believe that members will want to serve and that they have much to give. They do not feel that members need to be cajoled into service. They are confident that people can and will do what needs to be done, and somehow they communicate that confidence. They invite and encourage, but refuse to coerce. A simple "no" will be respected if a person for any reason does not wish to take on a responsibility.

"If I ask persons to take a leadership position," explains one pastor, "I don't run behind them and needle them about doing their work. I back off and let people follow through."

Again there is a significant difference in the responses from ministering congregations and from the Presbyterian Panel. Eighty-nine percent of the pastors and 79 percent of the elders in the ministering congregations say that members know that the church has high expectations for their commitment to and accountability for service. For the Panel, comparable figures were 56 percent and 55 percent.

Taking Membership Seriously

In at least two congregations in the study, the number of participants in activities is roughly equivalent to the number of members. Needless to say, that is an unusual ratio.

The pastor of the Green Estates Church explained why his congregation is so involved. "We have a lot of people who come who are not members. Frankly, most people come here for a year or a year and a half before they even join. They can join the first Sunday if they want to, but we don't play games with church membership. When I sit down with new members I share our history with them. We ask them to commit themselves to some kind of study, sharing, and serving. And we leave no doubt that we are really pushing toward sacrificial giving, which may be a tithe or beyond. And that is part of the commitment we expect when people join."

One couple, who have belonged to the Green Estates Church for thirteen years, were attracted there because of the challenge set before them by the former pastor. In talking about church membership, he made it clear that all new members were expected to study. When they hesitated, he pointed out that if they were not ready to commit themselves to such study, then they were not ready for "the Green Estates experience."

> "That pastor got us started. He expected that we were going to perform and there was no doubt that we would. He was not interested in numbers. He wanted a strong core of members."

More than one member of the Green Estates Church says: "What drew us to membership here was that the church meant business. There is an expectation that one will be involved from the very first. People are attracted to and join the church because they want involvement."

Adult to Adult Relationships

Another congregation in which participation outstrips membership is the Forest Canyon Church. In many ways their approach is different, but their expectations are also high. The pastor describes it this way:

> "The people who get integrated into the congregation tend to be on the assertive, extrovertive side. Immediately they are treated like adults and they are invited to use their own initiative and creativity. Those who are interested in exploring what membership might mean must take their own initiative to get the booklet from our staff people. The booklet describes what it is going to cost them if they get into our membership. Every few months we have a meeting for those who wish to explore the matter of membership further. After they have read the booklet, they come and their understanding of the booklet is clarified. There is one meeting and anyone who applies is taken in. There is no pressure. We bend over backward not to call people. People who join do so on their own initiative. If you take the transactional analysis categories of 'parent,' 'adult,' and 'child,' what we try to set up in the psychodynamics of our life is adult-to-adult rather than the classical parent-to-child relationship. People in

our community don't feel deprecated by either the minister or the session or other staff people. They are encouraged to use their own initiative."

Choice Is Important

Choice is an important part of the thinking of ministering congregations. They seek to give people many different alternatives for service. They actually encourage members to say no, if that seems to be an appropriate response. The pastor of the Northern Heights Church puts it this way:

"Our feeling is that when things are unstructured and people feel free to do as little or as much as they want to, they tend to do more.

"One of the things we discovered was that people feel guilty about saying no. So we announce that we would like to get a group of people together who are willing to offer personal assistance and support. We will put you on a list, and if for some reason you can't do it when a deacon calls, don't worry about it. No problem. Don't feel guilty. Feel free to say no, because there is always someone else on the list. We'll just go down the list until we find someone. When people are relieved from feeling guilty about something, and they know they can say no, if they have to, they are more than willing to say yes."

In other words, the high expectations that ministering congregations have for their members are not thrust upon their shoulders as burdens to carry, but rather are set before them as opportunities. The assumption is that they will serve freely and effectively. And they do.

Another pastor explained: "We always struggle with a way to talk about expectation so that it doesn't become a trip laid on somebody. I would like to think that we are coaching, shaping, and directing the response of people—that we are stretching them out beyond what they thought they could do, inviting them into a journey, into a pilgrimage and to an adventure, not being afraid to admit mistakes; or to deviate where we need to."

Sharing Vulnerability Naturally

The concept of grace becomes believable when the pastor demonstrates the meaning of grace in ministry. "Our pastor is human—she is approachable." "Our pastor makes himself vulnerable. We know he is one of us. He is struggling with the same things that we struggle with." These are typical comments from members in the ministering congregations.

Listen to members of the Pleasant Lake Church:

> "I think there is a difference in this congregation from other churches I have been in. I have never had anyone share weaknesses. Before I came here I never heard pastors share their struggles. Maybe we can spot a difficulty. But to have a pastor say, 'I am struggling with that, too,' is different!"

> "Our pastors have been very human. They have been willing to have clay feet and have felt free to fail."

> "When our pastor shared the struggles he was having in his own marriage, my wife and I found it was then easy for us to share."

An elder from Old First Church speaks:

> "Bob is a real person. He doesn't put himself on a pedestal. He's just as down-to-earth as any member of the church. You can talk to him about most anything. With some ministers you are careful as to what you say. He is not shocked by much of anything. At least, he doesn't act as though he is. And he makes you feel comfortable in saying whatever you want and in acting in whatever manner is most comfortable to you."

A Word of Caution

There are genuine dangers in sharing one's inner self too openly. There is a fine line between being fully human and trying to demonstrate one's humanity by self-revelation. Because Henri Nouwen's analysis overstates the other side of the argument, it may serve as a corrective to the quotations from pastors of ministering congregations in this section.

On the one hand, no minister can keep his own experience of life hidden from those he wants to help. Nor should he want to. . . . On the other hand, it would be very easy to misuse the concept of the wounded healer by defending a form of spiritual exhibitionism. . . .

Making one's own wounds a source of healing, therefore, does not call for a sharing of superficial pains but for a constant willingness to see one's own pain and suffering as rising from the depth of the human condition which all men share.[9]

Nouwen's words should make pastors pause and weigh carefully any style changes they are considering, to make certain that any new openness will be a natural expression of their humanity.

Pastors of ministering congregations do not parade their weakness as though to prove a point, but share it as a normal part of helping their people appropriate the resources of God's grace.

"I Blew It Last Night"

It is Saturday morning in Grace Church. About ninety senior citizens from the surrounding community have gathered for their monthly meeting. Several rousing gospel songs are led by a young high school teacher with a beautiful voice and an attractive personality. The people are obviously moved. The pastor is introduced and says, "I needed that!" He speaks of how each day around the dinner table his family share one good thing about their day. He tells of how his daughter shared her deep embarrassment at school, because she had had a seizure. The family gave her their support. Then, turning to the present, he says: "I blew it last night. I came home tired and got into a row with my kids. I didn't really listen to them, because I was so uptight over the way my day had gone." In that context he shares his experience of the resources of divine grace: "Our God is one who forgives all our iniquity. Thanks be to God, who gives us the victory. Christ has won the victory over sin, brokenness, lostness, fear and death."

Those who hesitate at such candor may well listen to the words of Henri Nouwen: "The great illusion of leadership is to think that man can be led out of the desert by someone who has never been there."[10]

Findings from the Presbyterian Panel indicate that over two thirds of members and elders believe that "church members want to see their pastor as a very human person like themselves, but with access to special resources." Forty-two percent of the elders of ministering congregations feel that their pastors give high priority to sharing their humanity in specific ways. This is in contrast to 28 percent of the Panel elders who feel that way.

Symbolic Identification

In symbolic ways some pastors make clear that they are not set apart from the rest of the people. Some will preach without a pulpit gown, without notes, standing on the floor of the sanctuary in the midst of the people rather than from behind a pulpit. The people catch the symbolism and appreciate it.

Saint John's Church is located in a low-income residential community within easy driving distance of a major city. Most of the members work with their hands in skilled or semiskilled occupations. The way the pastor identifies with them symbolically during the worship service has become a precious reality to them. This comes out in many different ways as one talks with members of the congregation:

> "Our pastor comes out from behind the pulpit—comes down into the congregation and gives his sermon among us. He speaks from his heart and not from prepared notes."

> "When a minister stands behind the pulpit it gives you the feeling of his being aloof."

> "Our pastor's sermons relate to everyday things. He is with it! He talks about my concerns. He is not talking down to me, he is talking on the same level."

The Forest Canyon Church is made up largely of professionals. Their pastor also preaches without notes, standing in the chancel. As in Saint John's Church, members feel that this symbolizes openness, vulnerability, and a close one-to-one relationship.

Spiritual Authenticity

There is clearly a place for pastors to share openly and symbolically their humanity and vulnerability. It is equally clear, however, that this must be done in a way that is genuine. It must be a natural expression of the pastor's personality. There is a fine line between openly sharing humanity and blatantly exhibiting it. Pastors of ministering congregations seldom cross that line.

For some pastors, the sharing of vulnerability is a conscious act. As one of them put it, "You get others to be vulnerable by sharing your own vulnerability."

The issue, however, is one of spiritual authenticity. Symbolic acts and public statements of vulnerability must be thoroughly consistent with the informal contacts that people of the congregation have with their pastor. Members of the Foothill Church express how they feel about their pastor:

"That one hour on Sunday morning tells you a lot about the pastor's philosophy and authenticity. Bill is talking that language and he is living that reality."

"He is not 'holier than thou.' You can approach him on a human level. He is not judgmental. You can express yourself openly."

"Even in error you don't hesitate to go to him and admit you need help. He is completely honest without putting you down."

"Bill is a human being who is not afraid to show his frustration, but at the same time a person who witnesses to joy and to success and to answers to prayer."

Authentic humanity is of course demonstrated in different ways by different people. It is shown, for example, in a pastor who is able to laugh at himself and his foibles, or who asks some of his parishioners to minister to him and his own needs. As one pastor said: "I got into a situation sometime ago where I was in a middle-years kind of crisis. I called up five men and told them that I was just lonely for male companionship at a deeper level. 'Would you meet with me every Saturday morning for a year,' I asked, 'just to be my friend? Just to talk about things that matter to me?' They did. I don't know how common that is, but I certainly rejoice in it here."

Another pastor tells of how he learned to accept his own humanity. "I used to have to be somebody. Many ministers feel they have to help or please others because they are unsure of themselves. I came to realize that Christ accepted me as I was. I didn't have to be something other than who I was. I could be most effective by just being me. This allowed me to accept others for their just being them."

It would be difficult to find a better summary than that which Henri Nouwen gives us. Pastors of the ministering congregations are indeed "wounded healers." They draw upon resources that enable them to care for their own wounds as well as the wounds of others. They make of their own wounds a major source of power.[11] They have entered into the vulnerabilities of their fellow human beings and through pain and self-denial have been willing and able to articulate their faith in such a way that it is at the disposal of those they serve. They have entered "the promised but dangerous land" and can thus tell those who are afraid what they have seen, heard, and touched.[12]

They have fulfilled their pastoral calling as they have been willing to put "faith and doubt, . . . hope and despair, . . . light and darkness at the disposal of others who want to find a way through their confusion and touch the solid core of life. In this context preaching means more than handing over a tradition; it is rather the careful and sensitive articulation of what is happening in the community so that those who listen can say: 'You say what I suspected, you express what I vaguely felt, you bring to the fore what I fearfully kept in the back of my mind.

Yes, yes—you say who we are, you recognize our condition.' "[13]

Thus, grace has its own contagious quality. Through the Spirit, grace that is shared at the deepest levels of life creates the caring community.

CHAPTER 4

Becoming a Caring Community

> You are now fellow citizens with God's peo-
> ple and members of the family of God.
> (Eph. 2:19, TEV)

Grace and community are intimately interrelated. One can hardly experience one without the other. Acceptance is experienced through relationships with others. And mutual acceptance is the fabric of community. The grace of the Lord Jesus Christ, the love of God, and the fellowship of the Holy Spirit are as much a unity in experience as the Trinity is one and not three. In Jesus Christ, God accepts us as we are. That is grace. Because God accepts us, we can accept ourselves and we can accept others. We experience the love of God. So we are able to love and be loved by others. Grace is the prelude to koinonia (fellowship or community).

We have been emphasizing one facet of that interrelationship: acceptance. Now we shall look more carefully at koinonia: the caring community.

I. The Congregation as Family

Ministering congregations are dynamic organisms of love in action. Members have a strong sense of belonging to a caring community. Repeatedly, when they are asked why they are involved in ministry they say: "We are a family. People care, so I care too." "I have experienced so much love from others in the family that I must reach out in love." "Members of a family care for one another. We nourish and support each other."

Frequently the sense of being a family is obvious to the visitor on a Sunday morning in warm relationships which are expressed within the worship service and in times of fellowship before and after it. Laughter, friendly conversation, earnest dialogue, the clasping of hands, the catching of the eye of someone across the room. This is true of large congregations as well as small.

Certainly this describes the Green Estates congregation, which worships in a large multipurpose room. The people sit on three sides of a rectangle, facing one another. Members openly express their love for one another in hugging. They have learned to share their deepest joys and sorrows. As one of them explained: "People who are not comfortable with intimacy may drop out; for intimacy is part of our involvement." Another said: "That which draws me to Green Estates is the support system. I feel as though I could go through most anything because of the support I get there."

The Family Face Death Together

Doris Peterson was dying of cancer. She was not intimately known by most of the members of the Green Estates congregation. One Sunday morning shortly before her death she came out of the hospital long enough to participate in the worship celebration. Her presence was a deeply moving experience to everyone.

On the morning of Doris Peterson's funeral two women of the congregation were in the church building. The funeral director expressed concern that there seemed to be no place to put the family where they would not be exposed to the view of the whole congregation. The two women allayed his fears. This congregation was different. People did not hesitate to share their feelings with others. "In our church," they explained "the family usually sit in the front row. In our congregation it is important for all of us to share the feelings of the bereaved family."

The Family Support One Another

As with the Green Estates congregation, the support that members in other ministering congregations give one another in time of deep sorrow or of high joy is a precious reality.

When you talk to people about why they are involved in ministry some say that when there was a crisis in their lives they found that members of the congregation really cared and extended them support. They share joys and sorrows. They know each other so well that each senses the needs of others. They tell how their lives revolve around the church. There, people are responsive, and strong friendships undergird them. One of them said:

> "This isn't a place where you come on Sunday and leave the rest of the world behind. This is part of our world. It's our family. The things that we do together, the sharing that we do, and the things that we look forward to, the rituals that we build up during the year, that we share as a family—that's what keeps me here, because this is my family."

Families Help One Another

Members of ministering congregations consciously link their motivation for service to their sense of belonging to the family. In a family everyone helps one another and you feel more free to ask others for assistance. So members of the family find many ways to show that they care for one another.

The Church Family Meets Basic Human Needs

Loneliness, isolation, and a sense of being enmeshed in the toils of merciless and impersonal corporate power are overwhelming emotions in our culture. Whatever experiences contribute to a sense of personal worth and to a relationship of caring love speak to deep human needs that, on the whole, are not otherwise being met.

High mobility has separated many persons from relatives and friends. Not only is the larger family a thing of the past but the nuclear family itself is threatened, and for many it is nonexistent. When the church has the characteristics of a warm and caring family it becomes an attractive option for many people. When congregations plan intergenerational activities, and opportunities for parents without partners or for singles to develop close personal relationships, they are meeting fundamental needs.

It is not strange, therefore, to have people explain their active relationship to a congregation with such words as these:

> "I moved here without a family. The first friendliness I experienced was in the church. A lot of couples and single persons like I was come here. We are by ourselves and we have energy and interest in the church. Compound that with the fact that we don't have family ties that place obligations on us, and this really does become a family unit to us."

Facing Socioeconomic Frustration Together

A shared experience of need is fertile ground for growth of community. Look at congregations whose membership is made up largely of people with low incomes and high levels of socioeconomic frustration. Members will frequently mention as reasons for their involvement in ministry the fact that they know the meaning of need in their own lives. Because they share the same problems as others in the community, they can empathize with their neighbors. It is natural for them to do what they can to meet the needs of the community.

Community in Racial or Ethnic Congregations

Identity with persons of a common cultural background becomes an important force in enhancing the sense of community within a congregation. The need which the whole racial or ethnic community shares becomes an important motivation for active ministry on the part of the people of God.

In a Mexican-American congregation the pastor said: "We

have a special ministry to our fellow Mexican-Americans. They need a leadership that we can provide, and we must provide it. Otherwise the future of Mexican-American churches is at stake. We feel that this is a time when we must do something. Because most of our church members come from Presbyterian families who have been Presbyterian for three to five generations, there is a meaningful commitment to a good tradition."

A Japanese-American congregation focuses its ministry not only on the immediate congregation but on the entire Japanese-American community, Buddhist and Christian alike. Whether it be advocacy for justice when Japanese-Americans are being discriminated against, or whether it be finding jobs for the unemployed, the Christian community has become the stimulus and the driving force within the entire Japanese-American community. The president of the Japanese-American Citizens Organization is a member of the congregation. The congregation is one of the main sources of support for that organization. The pastor explains that this results from a dual sense of identity: one with the racial or ethnic community and the other with the Christian community. The Christian perspective has enabled the congregation to surmount barriers that have been erected by subgroups within the community. It is Christian love which has enabled members to overcome the opposition that has come to them from various Buddhist groups.

The Family of God in Small Rural Communities

In small towns and rural communities, residents know one another well and may even be closely related by intermarriage. Everyone is familiar with the personal circumstances of everyone else. If anything, people may be too closely intertwined. In such circumstances, what makes for a caring Christian community? Certainly it is not just knowing one another well, nor having a sense of sharing a common heritage. It is the reconciling power of the Spirit of God that transforms close human contact into the family of God.

II. THE SPIRIT CONSTITUTES THE FAMILY OF GOD

All that has been said does not imply that the principal driving force in caring communities is related primarily to meeting human need. Caring communities are more than a sociological or psychological phenomenon. Lives are being transformed by the redeeming power of Jesus Christ. One is struck by the frequency with which people mention the power of the Holy Spirit at work in their congregations. In some congregations such comments refer to charismatic phenomena. But in more of them, it is the clear recognition that the reconciliation they experience and the responsive love they enjoy is the work of God, not just the work of the pastor or the session or the members.

The Fellowship of the Spirit

In the context of ministering congregations, the benediction phrase "The fellowship of the Holy Spirit" takes on new and rich meaning. It is the love of Christ, mediated by the Spirit, which brings the family of God into being. It is the Spirit that continually re-creates the quality of relationships among members of the family. This reality seems to be present even when traditional evangelical terminology has been discarded and other terminology is used to express the same experience.

This observation was perhaps most sharply articulated in Grace Church by a member of the staff. He felt it was the evangelical orientation and the openness to the teaching of the Holy Spirit which led the people to be ready to sacrifice and to give of themselves. As he put it: "They have a vibrant faith. People really love each other. They like it here and have time for each other. There is a lot of sharing of their lives with one another."

Two thirds of the elders in ministering congregations and more than three fourths of the pastors say they receive "very much" or "quite a lot" of help in living a life of service to others from the work of the Holy Spirit in their congregation. For elders in the Presbyterian Panel these figures are significantly lower.

Similarly, elders and pastors in ministering congregations are more likely than their counterparts in the Panel to say that members pray together in many different times and places about common concerns.

To illustrate the vertical dimension that is present in the caring communities, we might listen in on a conversation between several members of the Pleasant Lake Church:

"In the Inquirers groups and Koinonia groups, we have learned to respond to God's love. We look for Christ in other people. I had always thought of the church as a duty or an obligation. This has all been turned around. I began to respond to Christ not out of a sense of obligation. I respond to other people and seek him out in them. That is where you begin to relate to other people on a fairly deep level."

"I went through some forty years of my life ignoring the people around me. I treated them nicely, but essentially I did not become involved with them. But then I became sensitized and said, 'I simply cannot ignore people anymore.' It is not profitable. I see a world around me that does ignore people and my heart aches for them. They are missing one of the great joys of living. I was there. Thank God I am not there now. . . . Thanks to the help of a lot of people who have helped me to discover this new dimension. I see it all around me. Where did it come from? It is a gift. I don't know any other way to explain it. It is a blessing that God has given the people in this church."

The Unity of the Spirit

Another evidence of the working of the Holy Spirit in ministering congregations is the unity which they reflect even in the face of considerable diversity. Chapter 2 emphasized that they have a clear sense of mission which attracts like-minded people. Chapter 3 made clear that there is acceptance of diversity. Both are true. Marching behind the banners that fly are people of many different persuasions. But they are marching together in unity.

These congregations, like all congregations, must deal with conflict and stress. Conflicts offer the potential of creativity on the one hand or of disruption on the other.

A leader of the Green Estates Church tells of the explosive energy, the potential, the diversity, and the people power of that congregation. Their koinonia, their sharing, and their support groups keep them together. The congregation, she feels, makes it difficult for its ministers of the Word. "There are single-issue people in the congregation, and the pastors have to keep it all in balance. People are led in different directions. The pastors let us go, and play a role of healing, congealing, and tossing out new forms of involvement."

The pastor of that congregation puts it a little differently: "You can't have this diverse group without paying a lot of attention to individuals and where they are personally. You need to help a congregation see that it has its own healing power. It can have divisions. It can have disagreements. It can have conflict. And there is still a lot of power to take care of all that."

Old First Church draws people from the suburbs as well as from the highly depressed and deeply troubled neighborhood in which it is located. In addition to different racial and ethnic backgrounds, there are great socioeconomic differences among its members. A member of the session explains: "We are all one family. We are all brothers and sisters. This is one of the few places where you can see this in action. There is such a wide variety and range of people who trust and respect each other and get along in harmony. We cut across all kinds of boundaries, and everyone is able to participate. There are no power struggles that I am aware of. It's just a unique place!"

The Saint James Church has a similar diversity. An elder says: "There is a strong feeling of fellowship in this church which I think keeps people here. It draws them together and gets them involved. And they stay involved. If some of us don't agree with certain programs, the feeling of unity is strong enough that we just get involved anyway."

In other words, the unity that is necessary for fellowship is not dependent upon uniformity. It cuts across different dimensions of diversity. One cannot help thinking again of the Paul-

ine image of the body and its parts; of different gifts and of the
one Spirit that unites us all.

III. WORSHIP NURTURES THE FAMILY OF GOD

The worship life of ministering congregations creates and
forms the caring community. Worship on the Lord's Day is the
caring community gathered together in joyous celebration of
the love of God. It is communicating that love for each individual worshiper. It is warmth and intimacy and personal caring.
It is a time for the people of God to share in the personal joys
and concerns of members of the family. It is symbolic acts of
partnership between pastor and members. It is participation of
the laity in preparing and leading the service of worship. It is
the joyous weekly reunion with others you care for very much.
And it is learning to care even more as God's Word challenges
you to be all that God intended you to be.

Jesus Loves You

It is Sunday morning. The huge Gothic sanctuary of Grace
Church is filled to overflowing. There is an air of anticipation.
Children are the focus of the service. A child of five or six years
of age plays a Bach violin solo as prelude. The pastor welcomes
the congregation and a lay member of the children's committee of the session leads the invocation. A children's choir comes
forward and sings several gospel songs, closing with "Jesus
Loves Me." In preparation for the morning prayer the pastor
talks about members of "our family" who may be far away. He
reminds the congregation that they are engulfed in love and
asks that each worshiper clasp hands with the person on the
left and the person on the right. As they do this, he prays with
warmth and fervor, emphasizing the healing of hurts that people have brought with them into the sanctuary and the redeeming love of God in Jesus Christ. At the close of the prayer
he asks the congregation to sing "Jesus Loves Me." Then he
asks them to sing it again. This time they are to change the
words. They are to sing "Jesus Loves You" as they think of a

particular child for whom they want the love of Christ made real. He asks the congregation to remember in their prayers the family of a departed and much-loved member whose memorial service is to be held the next day. He tells of a young man of twenty-two who drowned in a recent accident. The service continues.

Give the Lord a Hand

It is another Sunday morning. This time we are in the Green Estates Church worshiping "in the round." There is a joyous choral call to worship. The theme of this time of celebration is our calling to service in the world. Love for the world is emphasized. As new members are received, deacons stand with the members from their parishes. A prayer of thanks for the new members affirms their "commitment, concern, and creativity."

Then comes time for sharing joys and concerns. Among those who speak is a man who shares news of the Caesarean delivery of his child. The anxiety has been great. Tears have been shed during the time of waiting. "But the Lord pulled them through." He closes by asking people to "Give the Lord a hand!" They do.

Another member stands to express the joy he and his wife share in celebrating their thirty-second anniversary. Perhaps, he suggests, he should ask the congregation to sing "Amazing Grace." There is spontaneous laughter. Instead, he asks that they sing "What the World Needs Now Is Love." The pianist has some difficulty playing it, since it is not well known. Never mind! The people sing lustily anyway.

Symbolic Acts of Partnership

Again it is the Lord's Day. At the appointed hour the pastor of the Foothill Church comes forward with a lay leader. They go to the first pew and kneel. As part of the worshiping community, they bow in prayer. Before going into the chancel, the pastor, standing on the sanctuary floor, welcomes the people.

During the sermon, he tells of a woman in the hospital he visited several years ago. She was critically ill and in great pain. "I have good days and bad," she said. "I have learned to take the day and give thanks for it." "She ministered to me that day," the pastor concludes. "I needed that. I was struggling with her situation. And she gave me more than I gave her."

When the time comes for special requests, a woman asks prayer for a brother sick in the hospital. The pastor talks with her a little about it. He turns to the congregation and asks, "Is Mary here this morning?" She stands and says, "I want to thank everyone for praying for me." Again the pastor speaks, "Cary, I believe you asked prayer for your father." And so it goes.

Before offering the prayer the pastor invites anyone who wishes to offer silent prayer for some special joy or concern to come forward and kneel. Five people come to the front pew which is reserved as a kneeling bench.

There is infant baptism. The clerk of session participates in the baptismal service. The pastor explains the vows to the parents. The clerk asks questions of the congregation. The pastor turns to the parents. "Do you have any friends you want to share with you in this?" They do, and the friends come forward.

Could anyone doubt that this is a caring community? Could anyone miss the heartwarming love? Could anyone fail to catch the symbolism of partnership in ministry?

Sharing of Joys and Concerns

Nearly half the ministering congregations invite the sharing of joys and concerns before the pastoral prayer during Sunday worship. As one would expect, this is more frequently done in congregations with fewer members. More than eight out of ten pastors of congregations with fewer than 300 members do this. However, approximately one third of the pastors in churches with more than 1,600 members also give such an invitation. In one large congregation prayer request cards are collected by the ushers during a hymn just before the pastoral prayer. And the pastor prays for each person by name.

Coming to the Microphone

The John Knox Church has approximately 740 members and is located within several blocks of the state capitol. For the past ten years the worship services have been open and participatory. The pastor says: "We have been evolving a worship experience that includes human contact and the exchanging of the peace. We join hands while singing the Gloria Patri. But most distinctively we have a microphone available following the sermon for the time of the congregational concerns and the prayers for the people. Either one of the ministers or a member of the congregation comes to the microphone and invites others to bring their concerns. People come to that microphone and mention a personal healing, or the need of somebody who is sick, or someone who has had a great joy. What is said can be as prosaic as announcing a meeting. During the Watergate period in the Nixon Administration that microphone became the focus of a great deal of conflict and controversy right during worship. But that was encountered and engaged within worship in such a way that the whole congregation was strengthened as a result of it. It's a powerful thing and has a way of building an enormous amount of trust."

Prayer follows the sharing in the John Knox Church and the pastor says that his pastoral prayers have never before been so meaningful. Worship in that congregation is at the heart of their self-identity and experience of ministry.

Lay Leadership in Worship

A common trend in many churches today is to provide lay involvement in the leadership of worship services. Often lay persons read the Scripture or make announcements. Ministering congregations differ in the amount of emphasis they place upon such lay involvement. Pastors and lay leaders collaborate in planning and carrying out the worship experience. Some pastors will have one or two lay "worship designers" assist them each week in planning the worship service. Or there may be a worship evaluation and planning group. The Northern Heights Church has a worship and arts committee which takes full responsibility for planning worship and for selecting the worship leaders. The pastor preaches the sermon and pronounces the benediction. Everything else is done by lay persons. Approximately one third of the members in that congregation have participated in leading worship over a period of three years.

In many congregations, not only will lay persons lead the worship services during the summer, they also preach the sermons while the minister is on vacation. Messages from lay leaders are not simply reserved for Laity Sunday.

Congregations with more than one service may have one contemporary service planned and conducted by a lay worship team. That service can be used as the occasion to involve increasing numbers of members in planning and conducting worship.

A Worship Team

Grace Church has involved members of the congregation in an extensive in-depth approach to planning worship services for this large congregation. The venture began when a call was sounded for persons who wished to explore the meaning of worship. Fifty persons came to the first meeting. For six months, those who were willing to continue the exploration met with the minister of music to talk about worship possibilities, and to contribute individual research on the traditional elements of the worship service. They met each week in intensive study. By the end of six months there were still about twenty persons active in the exploratory group.

At that stage, a decision was reached that ten participants would be chosen to be members of the worship team. The selection was to be preceded by prayer and consultation. Those selected would be asked to covenant together to spend at least five years on the worship team. This unusually long period of commitment was necessary in order to avoid the experience the church had had with groups in which creative persons worked on a project such as this and then "burned out" after a year. The worship team was asked to meet twice a month for three hours each time. The members of the team were told that one of the two meetings would be on a Saturday morning. This was a call for a high level of commitment!

Ten persons were selected, and accepted the responsibility. An effort was made to select a balanced group that had different gifts and represented different perspectives. The team did not begin to plan worship services for the congregation, but continued to meet for a full year. They worked closely together as a Koinonia group. They studied worship, visited churches, attended conferences and Christian art seminars, studied Avery and Marsh material, did homework, and worshiped together. Some were impatient and wished to get on with the task. But the minister of music encouraged them to be patient and to lay a solid foundation for their calling. Finally, after a year of preparation, the worship team went to the session. One by one they told who they were, what their gifts were, and "what Scripture had touched their hearts." Then they asked the session to examine them, to lay hands on them, and to delegate them with authority to prepare the worship services. This the session did.

Worship services for the congregation are planned by a member of the team in close consultation with the whole team. Sermon themes are secured as far in advance as possible. Pastors are asked to summarize their sermons in one sentence. Work on worship services begins at least one month in advance and an effort is made to integrate the whole worship experience with the Scripture and the sermon. The proposed service is completed at least a week in advance. It is then made available to members of the staff who will be taking part to discuss with all the participants.

After three years five or six of the original group still are part of the worship team. Six others have been added. New members went through a similar but less extensive training process, participated in exploratory meetings, and were then invited to make a three-year commitment to the team.

Preaching Makes a Difference

The crucial influence of inspirational preaching has been implicit in much that has been said about the role the pastor plays in articulating a vision for the congregation, making real the needs for ministry, and calling people to fulfill their ministries. Preaching is crucial in the nurture of the caring community.

More than three fourths of the elders in ministering congregations feel that they receive "very much" or "quite a lot" of help in living a life of service to others from Sunday worship services and sermons.

To get an idea of how important preaching is to many members, listen to a conversation between two members of the Green Estates congregation as they talk about how much their church means to them. "If you take my job out of my life," the one says, "there is not much left that is not in some way related to Green Estates." The other agrees, then asks him what would happen to the congregation without the sermon. They assume that the fellowship and the singing and the hugging and the sharing would all continue. Only the sermon would be discontinued. What would happen? Quickly both agree that all the other things that they prize so highly, and all the rest of the life of the congregation, would not last very long without the preaching. It is Christ at the core that binds that congregation together. Preaching relates them to Christ.

Whether or not all other ministering congregations would rate preaching that high, it is clear that a vital contribution of their pastors is the preaching ministry. Just as caring love is demonstrated and caught in these congregations, so also it is taught. It permeates the worship services, the times of sharing, and the messages from the pulpit. These pastors know how to communicate. They inspire and motivate and educate in their preaching.

Frequently the preaching in ministering congregations integrates the sermons with a churchwide emphasis over an extended period of time. It may be an emphasis on hunger or racism or spiritual renewal or community service or community action. Opportunities for adult classes are planned to enable people to explore different facets of any particular theme as they may be inspired to do so in the worship and preaching experience. Small groups meet to pursue possibilities which come alive through the proclamation of the Word. Then sermons lead people farther down the road of commitment.

One such emphasis made a lasting impact on the life of the John Knox Church. Inspired by Elizabeth O'Connor's book *Call to Commitment,* [14] the pastor preached on "A Call to Holiness" and invited those who might be interested in pursuing a disciplined spiritual life to come to a Maundy Thursday Communion service in the home of the president of the Women's Association. Those who came were deeply moved and agreed to form a Servant Company. The next evening, following the Good Friday service thirty-six persons gathered in the chapel and signed a commitment to the exercise of seven disciplines of the spiritual life: (1) regular corporate worship, (2) stewardship, (3) study, (4) daily prayer using a lectionary, (5) a Koinonia fellowship meeting once a month, (6) an annual retreat, and (7) a servant witness.

Following Easter there were three sermons on "An Easter People" and others were invited to come for conversation to the chapel after the service. The pastor looks back on the first year in the life of that small group of which he was a part, with rapture. "We felt an enormous love for one another, and almost everyone in that group went through an almost explosive ministry, on the school board and in the community." The Servant Company continued to meet for five years, and created an environment in which many things happened. In the pastor's words: "We never were perceived as an exclusive group. We were the tugboat for this ship. And the reality of that story is still feeding this congregation."

IV. THE FAMILY OF GOD REACHES OUT TO THE WORLD

The call that comes to the family of God is to be a *people for others.* The family of God reaches out in service to the world. That is the focus of its fellowship. Mission to the world is the reason for its existence. If that is so, in what ways does the intimate experience of Christian community prepare God's people for the outward movement of Christian ministry? The Servant Company, we are told, was consumed by rapturous love for one another. This resulted in an explosive involvement in ministry inside the congregation and out in the world where the servants carried on their work. A fellowship of Christians that cared deeply for one another and entered into a common discipline became a dynamic source of powerful ministry.

Cared for People Will Care for People

In ministering congregations one hears repeatedly that when members experience real caring they learn to care for others. Having experienced love, they are able to love. When needs are met, people are free to meet the needs of others.

The pastor of the Pleasant Lake Church puts it this way:

"A great many people in our congregation feel cared for and supported. We have a theme, 'Cared for people will care for people.' That is what I have found in preaching and teaching. If you have people whose personal lives are not at least meaning-fully addressed (the family life is unraveling, their personal sense of worth is not strong, their kids aren't making it, or their friend-ships are debilitated), it is pretty hard to ask such people to care about others. They are so caught up in their own personal needs that they cannot meet the needs of others."

Another pastor says: "It's just amazing! When people really get fed, and really get cared for, the other forms of ministry seem to form naturally."

The journey inward must precede the journey outward. Just as an experience of God's grace enables mutual acceptance in the community of the Holy Spirit, so is koinonia the fundamen-tal touchstone that releases the dynamic of ministry.

The Exercise of Ministry Does Not Come Automatically

Ministry begins within the fellowship of the people of God and then reaches out to all people. This is a *natural* progression, but it is *not automatic.* Love and gratitude experienced within the Christian community do overflow to the world around. But that loving response must be channeled by Christian teaching and effective leadership within the congregation.

Ministry in the world must be sustained from the base of Christian community. Robert C. Leslie is right when he says: "It is increasingly obvious . . . that bearing witness to the Christian faith today, in an essentially secular world, calls for a supportive community to venture out from and to return to for encouragement. It is doubtful that most people can be Christian without such a community standing back of them."[15]

On the other hand, one would have great difficulty establishing Leslie's other assertion: "Virtually any effort at deepening personal faith through sharing groups leads directly to a sharpened concern for outreach into the community." That may often be true. It certainly is not true invariably. Other factors enter into that translation of love into service.

The loving family which people experience in the congregation can easily become ingrown and self-centered. It can readily concentrate on satisfying the needs of the family members to the exclusion of those who are outside the immediate fellowship. Wise pastoral guidance and clear instructions are necessary to help people translate the love and gratitude they have experienced into community service and action on behalf of those to whom they are not related in a personal way.

Service in the community is encouraged by teaching and preaching which interprets the Biblical and theological understanding of ministry, makes the needs of the world real, and challenges members of the congregation to undertake specific ministries in the community.

Study Enlightens the Family of God

Characteristically, ministering congregations have a strong emphasis on adult education. One approach to Bible study gives attention to training lay leaders to teach the Bible to other church members. Participants commit themselves to one or two years of study. Classes meet for two or more hours a week, and students are expected to spend ten to twelve hours a week in preparation.

Participants must commit themselves at the outset to be willing to teach a class when they graduate. But teachers are selected at the conclusion of the course on the basis of their ability to teach. Lay persons selected then become the teachers of other classes of lay persons. In some congregations teachers recruit their own classes. In others people sign up for them as they do for other courses.

Most congregations offer a broad array of adult study classes. Often they are relatively short-term contract courses which require commitment to follow through with the whole program.

The Forest Canyon congregation plans its classes on a semester basis, similar in many ways to a community adult education program. In this 280-member congregation, as many as 250 registrants pay the class fee and enroll in one of the fourteen to seventeen courses given each semester. Many of the courses are taught by professionals. Included in the curriculum are classes in the theological perspective of the congregation, farm worker concerns, interpersonal relations, communications skills, and even auto repair. The internationalization committee sponsors an annual international study tour that goes to such places as Nigeria, Eastern Europe, South America, and Israel. Each tour is preceded by an intensive study course in world issues and international mission.

The John Knox Church cooperates with several other congregations in an ecumenical Lenten study program designed for members of the participating churches and people from the surrounding neighborhoods. One set of classes meets on Sunday evenings. Another on Wednesday evenings. Prior to enrollment, members of the youth groups of John Knox go from door to door in the neighborhood to give out brochures that describe the classes and invite participation. As many as half the participants come from the community. There are classes in Bible, theology, neighborhood development, criminal justice issues, and such other subjects as cults and religious movements, and the human potential movement. Instructors are lay members of the churches who have particular expertise or professors from the state university, campus pastors, and others.

Other congregations may offer courses in business ethics, legal ethics, medical ethics, world hunger, or family issues such as incest, child abuse, and runaway youth. Or they may sponsor an annual family gathering to which come several hundred members for four or five days. In a recent year one of these family camps asked members of the congregation who are involved in community agencies to educate the membership on the way in which their congregation was involved in the world around them.

One cannot deal adequately with the way in which study stretches the minds of the people of God without recognizing the important role that women's associations often play in awakening members of the congregation to what is happening in the world. At least one congregation depends heavily upon its women to do the programming in mission education for the church as a whole.

Study enlightens the family of God and enables its members to channel their caring love to the world in which they live. But first they must learn to care and to love. It is the Spirit that teaches us to care and to love. The Spirit comes to those who are gathered together in upper rooms. The Spirit comes to those who have all things in common. The winds of the Spirit are always blowing. In the intimacy of face-to-face relationships people learn to trust. Through the inspiration of open relationships people gain the courage to open the windows of the soul to let the Spirit in. In the face-to-face relationships of small covenant groups much renewal takes place within ministering congregations. Let us look at those groups.

CHAPTER 5

Renewal Through Relationships

> Day after day they met as a group in the
> Temple, and they had their meals together
> in their homes, eating with glad and humble
> hearts, praising God, and enjoying the good
> will of all the people. And every day the Lord
> added to their group those who were being
> saved.
>
> (Acts 2:46–47, TEV)

How does Christian community come into being? How do
ministering congregations encourage members to be open to
the transforming power of the Holy Spirit? How do people
become willing to risk deep-caring relationships—to admit
their vulnerabilities, and to share their personal and spiritual
resources?

These questions are not easily answered. But the ministering
congregations do provide us with valuable clues. By grace we
are reconciled to God and in turn to one another. Our acceptance as individuals enables us to accept each other. The Holy
Spirit, who calls Christian community into being, is nurtured
by worship. Preaching and teaching help channel caring love
to others outside the koinonia.

Now we must emphasize that renewal comes through face-
to-face interaction of person with person. The Spirit acts
through individuals who are helping one another to discover
the meaning of reconciliation and to be faithful to their calling
as servants of Jesus Christ in the world.

How Caring Communities Come Into Being

A congregation can become a loving, caring community only if there are face-to-face relationships between individuals as authentic persons. Close personal relationships, in turn, are possible only in a climate of trust and mutual support. Mutual trust is an essential ingredient if people are ever going to share their vulnerabilities with one another. Only in person-to-person interaction can we experience caring in our own lives. Through such contacts we can see others who model genuine caring and we can ourselves practice caring for others.

John Harris speaks of his own theology as a "theology of relationship" in which truth emerges "out of the deeds and relationships of people." He affirms that "the local church is a dynamic field of personal interaction meant to have the effect of making us more caring, more self-searching, more conscious of the riddle and mystery of life than most of us normally ever are."[16] God communicates truth through the lives of persons who live that truth. That is the meaning of incarnation. The extension of the incarnation is to be found most clearly in face-to-face relationships.

In his chapter on "Community," in *Life Together,* Bonhoeffer says: "God has willed that we should seek and find His living Word in the witness of a brother (or sister), in the mouth of man (and woman). Therefore, the Christian needs another Christian who speaks God's Word to him (or her)."[17] (Parenthetical words added.)

Ministering congregations know that renewal comes through person-to-person interaction and have discovered many different, natural, and informal ways to stimulate such interaction. Their efforts can be described as occurring in three general areas:

Through a wide variety of small groups

Through parish care programs

Through modeling of caring love by pastors and laity

I. RENEWAL THROUGH SMALL FACE-TO-FACE GROUPS

Almost all ministering congregations have small face-to-face fellowship groups where people can participate in mutual support, where they develop trust and experience intimacy. They study together, share together, pray together, and often serve together. Within such groups they experience the real meaning of acceptance, forgiveness, grace, and mutual ministry.

One of the greatest differences between ministering congregations and other congregations is in the opportunities they provide for small-group life. In replying to the Lay Ministry Questionnaire, pastors and elders of ministering congregations were almost twice as likely as pastors and elders in other congregations to say that this characterized their congregations. This was true for both large and small congregations.

In Large Congregations

In large congregations, the advantages of small groups are perhaps obvious. How else can members get to know each other intimately? The advantage of a large congregation is the quality and diversity of its staff, and the many different opportunities it provides to participate in its life and work. Small groups enhance those advantages by being organized around different common interests. They break down the size of the church and provide opportunities for personal friendship, intimacy, and the sharing of life.

In Small Congregations

In regard to smaller congregations, one may easily assume that small groups will not add much to the community life of the people. One of the attractions of small churches is that they provide intimacy and fellowship. Members feel that they are a family, and everyone knows everyone else. But the pastor of Hope Church, which is in a Midwestern town of under one thousand, does not agree.

"We are a church of 225 members, which isn't really large. But it's really impossible to care for all those people. We have a church where people try to be friendly, but after three years you could still be saying, 'Hi. How are you? It's good to see you.' And you never get beyond that. Without small groups, where people can learn and share from the heart, there is really no way to get the bonds of ministry going between people. It may not be possible to care for two hundred people. But if there are nine or twelve persons, you can do that. If there are persons who are hurting, you can really help them on that kind of basis."

Why Small Groups Are Effective

Small groups are the most natural way for people to relate to one another. These groups are less formal than Sunday morning worship services and they put individuals into natural colleague relationships. One pastor commented on life in the congregation:

"It is our informal worship, our small groups and Bible study that has provided a positive support for lay ministry. The defenses people have to hearing the Word of God in a formal setting are broken down in the informal setting. In formal worship people say, 'Of course you would say that, because you are the minister.' Through informal group worship, people serve one another, share in the leadership, are more conformable in sharing their own concerns and in hearing the concerns of others. They receive support from one another."

Robert Leslie summarizes findings from various studies to explain some of the reasons that small groups have proved to be as valuable as they seem to be.

Experimentation with small training groups has led to the conclusion that the small group of seven members is the most effective agent for transmitting knowledge in the shortest possible time. Therapeutically oriented personnel have known for a long time that half a dozen patients attached to a person who is naturally therapeutic, whether he be gardener or plumber or vegetable preparer, make more rapid progress than in almost any other setting.[18]

A Word of Warning

Small groups provide the avenue for Christian community to develop. They are essential in the development of a ministering congregation. However, we must take seriously Bonhoeffer's warning not to seek for our own ideal image of Christian community but to accept community as a gift from God —a Divine Reality rather than the fulfillment of a human dream.

The serious Christian, set down for the first time in a Christian community, is likely to bring with him a very definite idea of what Christian life together should be and to try to realize it. But God's grace speedily shatters such dreams. Just as surely as God desires to lead us to a knowledge of genuine Christian fellowship, so surely must we be overwhelmed by a great disillusionment with others, with Christians in general, and, if we are fortunate, with ourselves.[19]

A Wide Variety of Groups

No single pattern of small-group life characterizes all the ministering congregations. There are many different types of groups. Some meet only once to study a particular subject or issue. Others meet for a designated period to engage in Bible study. Some groups are primarily for personal sharing and spiritual growth. Others are organized around specific mission thrusts. Still others are friendship groups, where people get together periodically for fellowship, play, study, or worship. Some groups are formally initiated, others spring up spontaneously. Some are highly structured, others are loosely structured. Some congregations concentrate a good deal of effort on a particular type of group. Others encourage great variety.

The Green Estates Church has perhaps two thirds of its members participating in one of many kinds of groups, and a great deal of their common ministry takes place in those groups. Some members belong to more than one group, each centered around different interests. Some are "group hoppers." Others might stay in the same group for ten years.

We shall now look at the different kinds of groups found in

ministering congregations. For clarity we will list them in five clusters: (1) Covenant Communities, (2) Inquirers Groups, (3) Mission Communities, (4) Community Within the Working Groups of the Congregation, and (5) Other Group Activities.

1. Covenant Communities

The Servant Company, which had such a significant impact on the John Knox Church, was a covenant community. A group of fellow Christians committed themselves to form an intentional community with certain disciplines that bound them together. They met periodically to share with one another in fellowship, study, and prayer.

Covenant communities take different forms. One pattern is the Koinonia group. A number of the ministering congregations have been strongly influenced by the work of the Church of the Saviour in Washington, D.C., and by the concepts of the Inward and Outward Journeys. (See Elizabeth O'Connor, *Journey Inward, Journey Outward.*) A Koinonia group concentrates on the Inward Journey as preparation for the Outward Journey.

Koinonia Groups

The Pleasant Lake Church has over fifty Koinonia groups of eight or more members each, meeting at least twice a month. The pastor estimates that 70 percent of the congregation of 2,100 members has been involved for at least two years in a K Group, as they are called.

The name comes from the Greek word for fellowship or community. Members of the groups study the Bible or Christian literature, apply what they are studying to life, pray together, share their life experiences, and seek various ways to enable individuals to carry on their ministries. When they gather, they "report in." "How are you doing?" "What is happening with you?" they will ask one another. The pastor evaluates the Koinonia groups most positively.

"These groups enable members to share faith and open themselves to the whole dimension of being cared for in Christian

community. In the Koinonia groups we get heightened con-
sciousness of what it might mean to be God's person in the world
today.

"Groups will vary in effectiveness. Where they are effective,
they are tremendous. I have less counseling here for a church of
2,100 members than I did in a former congregation that had 600
members. This is because people are ministering to each other.
I see it particularly if someone loses a spouse or a relative. The
Koinonia groups gather around in caring and then in following
up."

Each Koinonia group is led by a lay coordinator who has
received six weeks of training and who was selected for the
Gift of Caring. Coordinators must draw people out, listen to
them, and keep in touch with them. Coordinators meet
monthly with one of the pastors. At that time they go over
the syllabus for the month, which has been prepared by the
pastor.

In one series, for example, all Koinonia groups were studying what it means for every Christian to be a minister. This was
coordinated with a series of sermons on the same subject. As
the pastor said in describing the program:

"The stress in the Koinonia groups, in the nurturing groups, in
all of our Christian education, is to equip people for their ministry of reaching out, caring, and recruiting. We feel that we are
not just nurturing people for their own benefit. It is in order to
impact family life, community life, work life, life in the nation."

Young people of the Pleasant Lake Church participate in
discipleship groups which are patterned after the successful
Koinonia groups but use different materials.

2. Inquirers Groups

Undoubtedly, the key to the success of the Koinonia groups
in the Pleasant Lake Church has been the Inquirers groups. All
new members must go through these before uniting with the
church. Even persons who have been church officers in other

congregations are expected to participate in the six weeks' Inquirers program.

As is the case with many suburban congregations, the Pleasant Lake congregation has a tremendous turnover in membership. The pastor estimates that over a recent ten-year period the congregation has taken in 2,000 new members and lost 1,800. It has been crucial to find some way to integrate persons quickly into congregational life.

The answer has been the Inquirers program. Of those who come to the Pleasant Lake Church, most have never used Scripture themselves, and have been nominal participants in church life. Many have experienced the church as institution, but not as Christian community. They do not know how to talk about their faith. In telling of the Inquirers program and of the K groups which follow, the pastor is justifiably enthusiastic.

> "For many of the participants, this is the first time in their lives they have been in a group of peers that has actually discussed the relationship of faith to their lives. Many have not even discussed the meaning of their faith with their spouses. This is for them the first taste they have ever had of Christian community."

Inquirers groups used to be led by one of the pastors. Now most of them are led by six teams of trained lay leaders. There are never more than twelve or fourteen in an Inquirers group. The number of such groups the church can have at any one time is limited by the number of available leaders. The session wants to train more team leaders to conduct these programs so that the church can be more aggressive in its recruitment program.

At the conclusion of an Inquirers group, participants are invited to continue as a Koinonia group. About 80 percent of the participants in the Inquirers groups choose to do so.

Without the experience of community they have had in the Inquirers group, most members would answer "No" to the Koinonia group. They wouldn't have time for it. But once they have experienced the fellowship, they make time for it! The pastor believes that many would not participate in the Inquirers group if that were voluntary. He is convinced that the session has been wise in requiring participation of all new church members.

The Impact of Inquirers Groups

The impact of Inquirers and Koinonia groups on the lives of individuals becomes clear when we learn what has happened to several participants in these programs.

> "This was the first time in some fifteen to twenty years of marriage that we had sat down and talked about what we believed about God and the Holy Spirit and the Christian community. The dialogue that took place in the six-week session gave us the opportunity to articulate some of our beliefs and to be comfortable talking about Christ and committing our lives to him.
>
> "We debated, we talked, we shared perceptions and feelings. We had questions that we had to respond to. We were then in a position to work in a K Group and continue this ability to verbalize; to pick up the relational kinds of ministries, and to affirm each other and to talk about gifts. It just became a much more natural life-style."

Renewal Through Peer Relationships

Koinonia and Inquirers groups are effective because peer relationships within those groups facilitate spiritual renewal. The witness of another church member carries weight that the words of the pastor may fail to convey. A member tells of his experience in an Inquirers group.

> "When we came to town we assumed we were going to live here for the rest of my working career. I prepared a list of churches and we set about checking them out. Since the Pleasant Lake Church was most convenient, we started there. We never went to another church. It was the aliveness of the people. The service was great, the size of the church a little overwhelming.
>
> "In the fall we joined the Inquirers program. The minister was dynamic. He said things that I expected a minister to say, but John Peters was there as a layman and he said things that were new to me. I respected him because, at that point, he had all that

meant anything in my life—a respectable job, a nice home, and a nice family. That's what counted to me. But that was not enough for him. I wondered what he was talking about.

"About the middle of those six weeks, one Saturday morning when I was standing out in front of our house, my youngest daughter and my wife were having a little go-round inside, which is normal for all families. I asked myself, 'What can we do to help this situation?' Suddenly I thought about the Inquirers program. Those folks were talking about prayer.

"I hadn't prayed since I was in second grade. One night at that time I did the daring thing of not saying my prayers before I went to sleep. The next morning I woke up and got through the day. And the next night I didn't say my prayers either. Then I didn't say them for another thirty years. That was the end of that.

"But these people were talking prayer. I'll try it. So I said just the most simple little prayer. 'What can we do to help Jane?' Instantaneously I got a little answer. Jane responds to love. Well, any psychologist can tell you that's no answer from God. But I wasn't so sure. And sure enough, we resolved that situation. Something else arose a few days later. I prayed about that situation. Lo and behold, as far as I was concerned I got another answer.

"By the time the six-week Inquirers program was up, I was able to commit my life to Christ. Not because of a minister, but because of a layman.

"Fortunately, I needed that for what came afterward. I went through a year and a half of hell in my work. As I mentioned before, my work meant everything to me. I took care of my family. But my goals were all work-oriented. Now I found that I could not work with my superior. He was a mental and physical cripple, and an alcoholic. I could not tolerate that situation and I actually told my superior that I was going to quit. Fortunately, I talked to a few more friends at church who told me that they had been there, too. With their support I made it.

"Think of the blessing that God gave me through that experience! I hadn't prayed in thirty-five years and now I prayed every night just to get through the next day. That is what did it. Not because of the ministers but because of the people in this church."

From Renewal to Social Action

Our third illustration from the Pleasant Lake Church portrays the step-by-step pilgrimage of one man from routine church attendance, through spiritual renewal, to active involvement in controversial social issues.

"A number of years ago I moved into town. As a matter of course we started coming to church. In the Inquirers group I learned that there is a living Christ I can turn to. This changed me and my whole attitude toward the church. The church challenged us to respond to the love of Christ. I was asked to work on youth programs, then on the session. Some members of the congregation were involved in sponsoring a housing project. They needed someone to serve on the board. From that I got involved in the Session Committee on Local Outreach and we in turn worked with the presbytery on a number of issues. For the last five months we have been dealing with the issues of civil rights for homosexuals. A number of years ago I would not have even wanted to talk about such a subject. But I have been studying various General Assembly documents and other documents dealing with the decriminalization of homosexuality, and our presbytery is now on record as favoring the protection of civil rights for homosexuals."

This man's personal pilgrimage models the way in which the Inward Journey can lead to the Outward Journey. Ministering congregations are concerned with both. And Koinonia groups can lead to mission groups.

3. Mission Communities

Koinonia groups often focus on the Inward Journey. We turn now to mission communities which intentionally focus on a common Outward Journey as well. The covenant they write with one another includes spiritual disciplines. They study, pray, share, and support one another. In addition, they commit themselves to work together in a particular form of ministry.

In the John Calvin Church in mid-America, one such group carries on a mission to divorced persons. They call their ministry Growing Through Divorce. As a covenant group they work on their own personal journeys in life and faith, and they carry out their ministry with divorced persons on Saturday night (a time that is particularly lonely for those who are single again).

A second mission group meets on Tuesday mornings for breakfast. On Wednesday evenings the members go to the penitentiary, where they meet with men who are open and committed to a spiritual journey. Their primary focus is on the body of Christ among those in the prison who already want to be people of faith.

Each of these groups has developed its own covenant. Covenants include ways in which participants will be open to the experience of God in their lives, develop their gifts through study, and share their resources with others.

Base Groups

Grace Church has developed the concept of covenant ministry groups into what it calls "base groups." These groups are seen as cells of the church's body which operate with all the basic functions of the church except the administration of the Sacraments. Each base group develops its own covenant which includes: (1) fellowship, (2) nurture, (3) worship, (4) "calling forth the gifts" of particular group members, and (5) a common calling to a specific mission or ministry.

The base groups were developed after a study of the work of the Church of the Saviour and after considerable experience with various small prayer and study groups. These groups were sustaining the individual ministries of church members but were not involving them in corporate ministries. Out of the initial study the first of several base groups was organized. That group began by seeking to discover the particular gifts that each of its members brought. The members then clarified their calling as a group. It was to encourage the establishment of other base groups among the more than two thousand members of the congregation. Within several years fifteen different base groups have emerged, largely out of the concerns of particular members.

A base group is usually formed by "the sounding of a call" to a particular ministry. A member who feels called to some form of ministry discusses this with one of the pastors or with one of the church officers. After permission is secured, a notice is placed in the church bulletin or the member is given time to make an announcement from the pulpit. Other members who wish to explore this particular form of ministry then meet at a designated time and place and discuss its possibilities.

The Loaves and Fishes base group was initiated through the concern of a minister's wife who felt called to do something about hunger. She talked to a number of persons who shared that interest and put a notice in the church bulletin. Twenty-eight persons responded and took part in an exploratory meeting. Out of these, sixteen to eighteen persons began to work together more intensively. A covenant was developed. The mission of this group is to alert the whole congregation to the problem of world hunger and to discover ways in which the congregation may tackle that problem.

The Loaves and Fishes base group has become involved in the community and in the other needs of persons who face hunger through poverty. It has moved beyond the narrow concerns of hunger to the social problems that contribute to poverty and hunger. The group is seeking ways to encourage the congregation to give higher priority to community concerns.

The Singles and Single Parents base group grew out of a call sounded by a widow who talked with one of the pastors about the needs for such a ministry. Twenty persons responded to that call. Of those twenty, six became members of the base group. They have covenanted for one year at a time to support one another and to carry on a ministry to single persons and to parents without partners.

Other base groups have been organized around ministries to college and career young adults, world mission, evangelism, and the training of fifty lay pastors for ministry in the geographical zones into which the congregation is divided.

4. Community Within the Working Groups

The sessions of more than one of the ministering congregations invest time in the relationships of their members with one another. Both the Pleasant Lake and the Grace churches begin each session meeting with a time of sharing. The individuals "log in" or catch up with each other. In groups of two or three persons they take at least a half hour to find out how things are going in the daily life of each. They talk about their families, their personal health, or their businesses. How are they doing in their Christian faith? Is there anything troubling them that might get in the way of the tasks at hand? They spend time in prayer for one another and then are ready to do the business of the church.

Task Forces and Committees

In place of base groups, other congregations encourage their task forces or committees to spend time in study, fellowship, sharing, and mutual support. Committees may meet in homes and relate to one another as people who share in a common pilgrimage of life.

The leadership of Grace Church believes firmly that every meeting of any committee should begin with a time of personal sharing and prayer. The life pilgrimage of each individual is taken seriously.

A typical committee meeting at Grace Church may spend half its time "in worship, caring, loving, healing." The leaders of the congregation believe that the work of its committees is done much more efficiently and effectively because of the time spent together as Christian community.

In like manner, where there are multiple staffs, ministering congregations find that it is crucial to develop a similar experience of community in depth which binds them together in their mutual responsibilities.

5. Other Group Activities

The number and variety of group activities in the ministering congregations is too vast to itemize. However, several approaches are significant and should not be passed over.

An Adoption Program

One congregation has developed an informal Adoption program. The pastor encourages members to relate on a sustained basis with five to eight other persons. He preaches and teaches that everyone is called to be a minister to others. He points out that, whether or not you belong to a small group, you can find several persons whom you can adopt or be close to. You can minister in a special way to those individuals, keeping in touch with them, letting them know that you are there to help. You can concentrate on a few people and do what you can to minister to one another. Perhaps three fourths of the members of that congregation have adopted at least two or three other persons. It may be one young mother who finds three or four other young mothers. They check in on each other on a regular basis, and help each other with baby-sitting. It may be a husband and wife who have adopted a couple who are senior citizens.

Suppers Eight

The Garden Hills Church has developed a program called Suppers Eight. Over a period of five or more weeks the pastor preaches a series of sermons on prayer or forgiveness or trust. On the evening following each sermon, twenty to twenty-five groups of adults meet for supper in homes. Each group, of eight to ten persons, is provided with copies of the sermon. In addition, the pastor has prepared a suggested outline to guide their discussion. Discussions are closely related to the theme of the sermon. Groups also participate in various "exercises" designed to develop their interpersonal relationships, broaden their understanding of the faith, and build the kind of trust that enables participants to take further action steps. Each week the groups meet in different homes.

By the end of the series, the groups have grown into closely knit communities. A few may continue to meet on their own. Usually different groups are organized for the next series of supper meetings, perhaps within the same clusters or geographic areas. This, in turn, builds greater strength within the cluster groups. It prepares a larger number of persons who know each other well enough to work together in service task forces when something needs to be done.

Intergenerational Life Together

A number of the ministering congregations give high priority to intergenerational activities. Much of the educational program of the Green Estates Church is planned on an intergenerational basis. Persons from age three to eighty or over meet on Sunday mornings in study, fellowship, and sharing communities for three or four weeks at a time.

Two or three times a year the congregation plans an intergenerational dance and music production. Children are paired with adults who are not of their own family. The participants may create their own costumes or plan different parts of the production together. As many as 125 may be involved in one of these productions. Lasting relationships develop between participants.

Extended Families

The Forest Canyon Church, on the other hand, has organized six different Extended Families of eighteen to twenty-three persons each. Each extended family is carefully constituted to include persons of different ages and family situations. There will be perhaps four different couples with their children together with four or five single individuals, parents without partners, etc. Extended families meet once or twice a month for fellowship and to celebrate holidays or special occasions such as anniversaries or birthdays. Since many of the members of Forest Canyon do not have relatives nearby, these extended families fill a need for a larger family context. Many of their activities are recreational in nature. From time to time the adults may meet to study or share with one another. This congregation also holds congregation-wide intergenerational celebrations keyed to the seasons of the church year. It has a large participation in an annual family camp program.

Family Clusters

The Trinity Church has a more highly structured intergenerational program. It organizes extended families of twenty to twenty-five persons from all ages and life situations. They are carefully recruited in a two-step process. First their general interest is explored and they are given information about the program and its expectations. Two or three leaders of the family cluster then visit in the homes. Participants are asked to commit themselves for ten weeks to meet for a meal, a learning experience, and fellowship. The first ten weeks focus on building a community of support where persons trust each other and share openly. Participants learn about communication systems and "rules" for living within families.

The second ten weeks, which most participants elect, concentrate upon developing relationships between life-style and global issues. Persons try to become more conscious of how their daily habits relate to a world of hunger, poverty, widespread suffering, and limited resources. Within that context they seek to be intentional about developing their own life-styles. For example, they make contracts to try to change their habits of eating or of energy use.

Thus the Trinity congregation combine in one program opportunities for more intimacy in developing personal relationships with opportunities to grow in their understanding of the world context within which their ministries are carried on. Children get to know adults. Teenagers develop friendships with persons of grandparent age. Together they have increased their concern about global issues.

Wholeness and Healing

Ministering congregations do therapeutic counseling and have healing group activities in varying forms. There are groups like Alcoholics Anonymous and Alanon, and other programs related to alcohol or drug dependency.

One congregation has ten or twelve members who have invited into their families persons whose lives have been deeply broken. These Extended Households, as they are called, provide a therapeutic family context within which those persons may rebuild their lives and discover wholeness again.

Creative Christian Community is a type of therapeutic program that one congregation found effective in transforming the lives of some of its members. Several years ago the leaders of that church became convinced that many small groups avoided personal confrontation and were too saccharine in quality. Accordingly, the church leaders spent a year training group leaders to facilitate creative confrontation aimed at personal and spiritual growth. Through careful training and supervision, they seek to bring together in the small-group process the insights of the social sciences with the faith commitments of the Christian community.

Marriage Encounter groups have played an important role in at least one congregation in developing open and trusting relationships which are so crucial to Christian community.

Occupational Groups

With all the variety of small fellowship and support groups that exist in these congregations, it is surprising that there were so few examples of occupational groups. One would expect that ministry within one's occupation would require opportunities for those with like problems to share their struggles to live out their Christian faith on the job.

In only a few congregations were such groups in evidence. Notable among these was the Pleasant Lake Church. As part of an extended churchwide emphasis on the Ministry of the Laity the members of the congregation developed a pilot project in which they organized several occupational groups. Each was to meet weekly for six weeks. There were groups of professors, physicians, social workers, and business persons. The medical doctors found it impossible to arrange their schedules—they were too busy.

The social workers faced similar difficulties but solved them by meeting at six thirty in the morning. They felt that their time together met some of their real needs for mutual support as they sought to discover how their Christian faith can be related to helping the poor and disadvantaged. The system, they felt, often did not allow any place for their faith.

The business group met regularly for lunch and continued beyond the six weeks' experiment. They developed close relationships, mutual respect in spite of their very different business situations, and provided each other with considerable support.

In contrast to the sparsity of occupational groups, the frequency of the Koinonia type of group which cuts across occupational lines suggests that relationship needs are better met in diverse rather than in homogeneous groups. Perhaps people in the same occupation are too close to their work to be able to stand back from it with others in that occupation and seek answers to their occupational dilemmas. This is one of the troubling discoveries from this study. It deserves considerable attention if the ministry of the laity in the world is ever going to have the occupational relevance that we believe it ought to have.

II. Renewal Through Parish Care Programs

More than two thirds of the ministering congregations have Parish Care programs of some kind in which members of the congregation formally minister to one another. The congregation is divided into clusters, zones, neighborhood groups, or care teams. This is often, but not always, on a geographical basis. Leadership for each cluster is provided by an elder, a deacon, or another member selected and trained for the task. In most such programs, parish shepherds are responsible for visiting their flock on a regular basis and for keeping in touch through a personal visit or by phone. In addition, they are concerned for ministry to shut-ins and are especially alert to opportunities for ministry during times of illness, death, family stress, or personal crisis. Shepherds may be active in sponsoring new members from their geographical area who unite with the congregation. At minimum, they are expected to alert the pastor to special needs for professional ministry. More notably, however, they are trained to provide the needed ministry themselves.

Conceptually, these small groups of several families are considered a mini-congregation. In a large proportion of these plans, certain group activities are also a part of the life of these caring communities. There may be parish meetings, or other special activities once or twice a year.

In some cases a cluster will be assigned responsibility for a churchwide activity. This gives members of the cluster the opportunity to work together and thus get to know one another better. A more modest approach may involve assigning to a deacon or a trained lay person the responsibility for the pastoral care of a particular shut-in.

Care Teams

The Calvary Church, in a Midwestern farming community with a population of less than 3,500, has an active Care Team program. Team leaders invite persons to special events in the church and alert the pastor to members who have special needs or who have been absent from services for several weeks. These mini-congregations aim to develop small support groups who will care for one another.

Project Hope

The young people of the Calvary congregation are involved in Project Hope, a program designed to provide help for people in emergencies. All the elderly and shut-ins of the congregation have been assigned to teams of young people. The young people call their flock regularly to find out if there is anything they need. They offer to run errands, particularly in times of emergencies which often come during the winter months. Thus, young and old develop meaningful personal relationships and the elderly can be confident that someone will be in touch to take them to the doctor, get medicine, or help meet other emergency needs.

Lay Pastors Program

Several years ago, the session of Grace Church became convinced that the only way to ensure a consistent caring ministry for every member in this large congregation was to divide it into groups of eight to ten families. Each group was to be served by a team of carefully selected members who would be trained and committed to serve as lay pastors to that flock. Under the guidance of a new staff member called for that purpose, a base group committed itself to developing a Lay Pastors program. The base group studied other lay pastoral ministries programs, developed a plan of organization, and decided how many lay pastors would be needed.

They initiated a pilot program in which members of the base group served as lay pastors for several experimental flocks. One flock was made up of single women. Their lay pastor was a single woman. The other flocks were randomly selected from a list of active members living within the same ZIP Code areas. Thus they were able to try out different patterns of lay pastoring.

Out of its experience with the pilot program the base group established the following minimum commitments for persons who would serve as lay pastors:

1. To make contact with the families assigned to them at least once a month (normally by a personal visit, occasionally by phone).
2. To pray daily for each individual assigned to them.
3. To make themselves available when needs arise.
4. To provide a good Christian example to their flock.

A class of over one hundred persons was organized to help participants understand some of the dynamics involved in pastoral care. Out of each class the goal was for thirty persons to commit themselves to a ministry of listening, caring, regular contact, and prayer as a part of this lay pastoral ministry program. One important need is for those who are involved in these pastoral ministries to have pastoral support. All lay pastors are assigned to other lay pastors to help meet their own pastoral needs.

III. Renewal Through Models of Caring Love

How is it that face-to-face relationships are so fruitful in opening the door to involvement in ministry? One important reason is that within those relationships people discover others whose loving and devoted service inspire them to go and do likewise.

The ministering congregations frequently mention the way pastors or lay persons have served as models of caring love. From such models others learn to demonstrate their love too. Caring love is more readily caught than taught. This is why face-to-face personal interaction around issues of faith and challenges to service play such an important part in the life of ministering congregations. Small groups provide people with opportunities to get to know one another well enough that the contagion of caring love has time to catch hold. The subject deserves further elaboration.

Pastors as Models

Christ himself is the supreme model of ministry for every Christian. But fellow Christians are models, too. Frequently the pastor is perceived as a model of caring love. "Look how Mary cares about the people of our community," say the people in the Covenant congregation. "How can I care any less?" When a local hospital official is asked how it happens that the people of the Covenant congregation are so involved in service to the community, she replies: "Well, you've met Mary, haven't you? Would you ever forget her?" Another says: "Look at her enthusiasm and dedication. She meets people where they are. When she enters the hospital, the lobby lights up. We were like wilted flowers when she came to us. She watered us, and we came alive."

Parishioners join in. "Our pastor spearheads things. Her drive sets the example that motivates us. She gets people to do what they ought to be doing." "Her inspiration, her outgoing personality, her encouragement, make you feel that you are a part of something, and you have to work." "She makes it go. Her devotion has rubbed off on us. We do these things now because we want to."

A Deliberate Strategy

Ask this dynamic sorce of compassion about her philosophy of ministry and she will say:

> "I never ask my people to do anything that I would not do myself, for one thing. I try to be supportive. I get personally involved.
>
> "When a ministry is in the infant state where people need to know that they have support and encouragement I'm going to work right along with them. But as the project develops, I try to back out as soon as I can. When we get to the point where the laity can completely carry the ball, then I can pursue other ministries. As soon as I can, I turn things over completely to the laity, which is where it belongs. Then I like to fade out of the picture."

It is clear from this pastor's comments that she consciously chooses to lead by example. But she does so only long enough for others to discover the thrill of taking part in meaningful service. Then they also become models of caring love.

Bill Stevens of the Foothill congregation makes modeling of service a conscious part of his strategy. Some things he does are acted parables to teach people the meaning of their faith. This is part of his natural style of ministry. For that reason it makes a powerful impact on those who know him. "Bill has a gift of loving people," says one of the parishioners. "We know he would welcome us if we called him in the middle of the night. I had an operation at six A.M. He was there, as he had been the night before. He just held my hand, and I knew that everything would be all right." Once a person like that shows concern for you, that concern passes off to you and you care for others too. It makes people want to contribute what they can.

In Small Congregations

Modeling can be particularly effective in the small congregation. Also it seems to have greater weight in congregations with higher percentages of craftspersons, salespersons, or those who are retired. Saint John's Church has less than 115 members. Most of them work in the skilled trades. They see their pastor as an important key to their own responsiveness to opportunities for service in the community. "Pete takes care of his flock. If he cares that much, we also should care." "Pete is a model. He is involved in a lot of community things. He is always available. He has a sincere love for other people in the community. He is concerned because people are suffering. We care because we see him caring."

In Large Congregations

The importance of the pastor as a model of caring love is not limited to small congregations. In ministering congregations of all sizes, elders are much more likely than in the average Presbyterian congregation to say that they receive much help from their pastor "as a model of Christian service." There are notable examples of pastoral models in large congregations.

The Pleasant Lake congregation has over 2,300 members. For many years that church was noted for its preaching ministry. Today it is a different congregation. Preaching still plays an important role in the work of the pastor. But now, the people themselves are absorbed in ministry. When you ask them how this came about, they tell you of a new pastor who came to them many years ago. His warm love for people and contagious caring became an inspiration to them. He was seen as a model of caring love in his preaching, in his teaching, in informal contacts with people, in his work with small groups *and* in his pastoral ministry.

Pastors of ministering congregations are people-oriented. They spend time with people where they are in the community. They talk with them and listen to them. They share themselves as persons and take time to be a friend. They are particularly alert to moments of special need. As one of them said: "I do a lot of crisis care. In times of need I go overboard in ministering to the people so that there is a real level of caring. People sense that. They know I care. I have as much direct contact with people as possible."

Modeling by Lay Leaders

In many instances lay people are also seen as models of ministering love. Where such models are evident they make a powerful impact upon the lives of other lay persons. Most church members assume that the pastor will be a caring person. That is what he or she gets paid for. But to discover active love in the life of a fellow member is quite another matter.

In the Saint James congregation, when people were asked to explain their involvement in community service, they repeatedly gave the names of three or four women of their fellowship who had demonstrated contagious caring. Marie is no longer living, but they look back to her dynamic service as a source of much of their current ministry. Describing her devotion to the disinherited of the neighborhood, they told how she worked to encourage others to join her in her ministry. She had a passion for the community which was irrepressible.

Constantly she was out among the people. She would take people with her as she visited in the homes, so that they too could catch the vision she had caught. She was noted for her compassion and was dearly loved by everyone. She communicated broadly throughout the congregation, lighting little fires wherever she went. The congregation had been involved in overseas mission. "Our neighborhood is mission," she preached, and organized a Head Start program with volunteer help. People would gather clothing and furniture and spend their time in teaching. She persuaded others to start a food cupboard. Anybody would do anything she asked. She was a model for ministry!

Men in that congregation also caught the vision. One invited Joan Smith to go with him into the community to help in one of the projects of the congregation. She is still at it. Through

Joan's leadership the congregation became the catalyst for starting a community center. The congregation had already succeeded in getting the community to take full responsibility for the Head Start program. But there were youth on the streets. Drugs were a menace. More action was needed. Joan's vision and commitment inspire many others in the congregation. She too takes others with her into the community so they may see, and hear, and get involved. She too has become a center of contagious love. But she is not alone. "We have many vocal doers," says a member of the session. "They speak up and insist that they be heard. They call people to responsive service."

In many different congregations the illustrations could be multiplied. A pastor tells of women in his church who "just somehow sniff out people with need," women who are "always doing some beautiful little things for these people." In a Hispanic congregation of the Southwest the members talk of women missionaries who used to serve the community center. Their loving service made many want to get involved. These early missionaries were giants of dedicated compassion. They made a lasting impact on many young women and on the children who came to their kindergarten.

Women of the ministering congregations frequently play important roles in developing vision for mission. They study crucial world issues and often lead the way to active lay ministry. Any strategy within the congregation that does not give women an imporant place would be shortsighted indeed.

Strategic Modeling Awakens to Ministry

Leaders, like Jane and Bill or Jean and Marie, deliberately use modeling as part of their strategy for getting people involved in ministry. We have seen this as they have shared their vulnerability along with the resources of God's grace or as they have acted out parables of caring love. They themselves have become instruments of God's grace. In all candor, and without pretense, they have learned to share themselves as they really are, with all their strengths and weaknesses. They are not pretending to be what they are not. But neither are they, with false modesty, pretending that they are not what they are. They are aware of the gifts they have been given and they are using those gifts. They love people, and relate effectively to them. Therefore, it is a natural part of their way of working to use their gifts of compassion, concern, empathy, and love with the intention of awakening similar gifts in others.

Renewal of the people of God comes through face-to-face opportunities for authentic relationships which reveal the gifts God has given us.

Renewal comes where a climate of acceptance and trust gives freedom to be honest with one another about fears and failures, about vulnerabilities and longings. It comes where receptive reconciliation can be experienced within the context of Christian community. It comes where gifted persons minister to gifted persons and become the vehicle for the Spirit's work. Where together God's children can discover God's purpose for their lives. Where together they can learn the courage and the compassion and the perseverance to accomplish that purpose.

CHAPTER 6

Using the Gifts God Has Given

Having gifts that differ according to the grace given to us, let us use them.
(Rom.12:6)

Ministering congregations have discovered how to free people to express caring love in ways that flow naturally out of their concerns, and that fulfill their potential. Leaders of these congregations have an almost uncanny ability to identify the gifts of the members, match those gifts to challenges for ministry, support people as they use those gifts, and cultivate those gifts so that people grow as they minister. One pastor put it, "I am the midwife to ministry—identifying the needs of people, helping them share their dreams, and then helping them to discover how to make their dreams come true."

Gifts of the Spirit

Ministering congregations believe that God gives the church the gifts it needs to fulfill its mission in the world. Ministry is shared by all out of a deep conviction that the necessary abilities to carry out that mission do not reside only in a few persons, but are present in many different ways in all members of the congregation.

There are different gifts, but one Spirit binds them together. The body has many parts and each part has its particular function. In an ultimate sense, only the head of the body can know how all the parts fit together. In that sense there is an underlying mystery about the gifts we have been given. We may never fully be aware of the gifts we possess. But because the Spirit constitutes the body, we do know that in each part resides the potential of fulfilling whatever functions the body may ultimately require from that member of the body. The Spirit calls forth these gifts.

Each member has received the particular gifts and talents needed to carry out particular ministries in the church and in the world.

Talents have been given us to be used. Therefore it is the responsibility of the people of God to discover what gifts every member has and release those gifts in the fulfillment of God's purposes. This is our fundamental stewardship of all that God has given us.

Not every congregation would describe this reality in exactly those words. But the theme is common to all of them. In Grace Church there has been a fairly strong charismatic movement. The pastor speaks of the gifts of the Spirit in terms that are familiar to that movement.

"We believe that the Biblical plan is that God's people are a gifted people. We believe in the gifts of the Spirit. We don't believe that the only gifts of the Spirit are tongues, or healing, or miracles. But we believe that every Christian receives the charismata, the gifts of God, and all are to use their grace gifts for the body. And so our calling is to call forth those grace gifts.

"Five years ago I began to major on calling forth the gifts of the staff, instead of having them fulfill my dreams. Since then they have begun to call forth the gifts of the lay people and they in turn have begun to call forth the gifts of other lay people. So we have three hundred to five hundred lay people who are in the ministry. I have never seen anything like it!"

Other congregations, where the charismatic flavor is not so evident, might describe the Spirit's work in less traditional terminology. Nonetheless they affirm that the people of God are gifted and recognize their responsibility to discover and make use of those gifts.

Believing in People

In many different ways, leaders of ministering congregations communicate to members that they are important and that their gifts play a vital part in God's work. If every member of the body is gifted, then every member has the capacity to carry out creative ministries. It is assumed that members want to serve and to make use of their gifts. All they need is a good opportunity to do so.

People are given responsibilities in the confidence that they will fulfill them. Then they are allowed to follow through. Because others believe in them, they discover they can do things they never thought possible. As one pastor remarked: "Various people of ability in our congregation have felt that in other situations they were stifled by the pastor. We work hard to respect people's integrity and the integrity of committees. We say to them 'O.K., you have a job, you carry the ball. We are here to help. We are the resource people.' "

How Gifts Are Developed

How do leaders of ministering congregations develop the gifts of their members? A vignette of the John Knox Church summarizes it beautifully.

The pastor talks to every person who has been asked to take a major responsibility. He discusses what will be expected and offers his support.

One of his parishioners was hesitant about accepting the presidency of her local women's association. "I don't think I can do it," she said. "I think you can do it," he replied. "You can use your own style." She accepted the task and did it well. Sometime later the church was looking at issues in criminal justice. She came to her pastor and expressed a deep concern for criminal justice reform. The pastor said, "Why don't you do something about it?" He suggested others who might join her in setting up a task force and helped her find resources for their work. The success of this task force led to wider involvement of other congregations and to her employment as their representative in the state capital.

What did this pastor do? He took time to work carefully and personally with a potential leader of the congregation. He was responsive to her feelings. He sensed her anxiety about taking new responsibilities. He encouraged her to do it her way, and gave her timely support. He monitored her pilgrimage and sensed when she was ready for a new challenge. He informed his congregation about issues of consequence to which the members might respond in ministry. He was a catalyst, helping his parishioner to develop a plan of action that would enable her to move forward into a new ministry when she expressed her readiness to do so. He linked her with others of similar interests. He let program possibilities emerge out of her sense of urgency to do something about criminal justice reform. He helped her put it all together, but he left the choice of what she would do in her hands.

The pastor of the John Knox Church develops the gifts of the members of his congregation because that is one of his top priorities. Members call him "coach." Whereas this may be said with a smile or in jest, it does represent the pastor's style. It is the people who are playing the game. His ministry finds fulfillment in the growth and effectiveness of the individuals and in the development of their leadership potential. In this, he is like the pastors of other ministering congregations.

Elders of ministering congregations were much more likely than other elders to say that their pastors give high priority to developing confidence and feelings of self-worth in church members and to encouraging the use of members' gifts.

A Focus on Equipping People for Ministry

Equipping members for their ministries is the principal task of both pastors and elders. Of course, this is corollary to the conviction that ministry is the work of all the people. If indeed it is true that the basic responsibility for ministry rests upon every baptized Christian, then the clear responsibility of leadership in the church is to help members identify their gifts, develop those gifts, and make use of them in ministry.

The pastor of the Foothill Church says: "If there is going to be any vital ministry operative in Foothill, it has got to be as a result of people who have been prepared for their task. I often talk of my role as a resource person. I am available to do whatever is necessary to equip people to do the job. So I do a lot of teaching, and I spend a lot of time in leadership development."

The idea of "enabling" has become almost a cliché. Many pastors say their task is to enable the people. However, the real question is how central that equipping task is in the way the pastor actually spends his or her time. Is it pervasive of all that the pastor says and does?

The staff members of one congregation discovered that they had to make this a central criterion in evaluating their work. The pastor reports on their experience.

> "I believed in equipping the people for ministry and I was equipping them in general. Dr. Roberts, a lay member of our staff, pressed us on how many of us were actually equipping people for ministry. He challenged us to evaluate our ministries on the basis of whether or not they were equipping people. We agreed to this. During the first year the challenge was done gently. But by the second year we were evaluating ourselves rigorously on those guidelines. We have come to have a total commitment to equipping the laity for their ministries and we have been majoring on equipping them rather than on doing the ministry for them."

Responsiveness Is the Key

Leaders of ministering congregations develop a style of leadership that is responsive to the needs and dreams of members in their congregations. They know their people, their concerns, and what issues are important to them. They know where they are going and learn of their dreams.

At the same time the leaders are responsive to the needs of the members of their congregations and the issues that confront the communities in which they serve. The pastors relate those issues to their own understanding of the gospel. As one pastor points out, it is extremely important to "identify points where ministry can and should take place, both within the congregation and in the world. This requires listening in order to identify needs, concerns, issues, and then making specific plans for responding."

Leaders are responsive at the same time both to people and to opportunities for ministry. Thus, whenever they catch a glimmer of concern on the part of some church member, or a hint that someone may be prepared to enter a particular form of ministry, they are ready to help facilitate the development of such a ministry.

Responsiveness is the key. Initiative is rewarded not only by the pastor but by others in the congregation. The ideas of individuals are taken seriously whether or not those ideas are ultimately implemented. In the Green Estates congregation a suggestion may be rewarded with a hug. Or the pastor might say: "I think that's a grand idea. Why don't you do it? Let me know how it goes."

A social worker in the Pleasant Lake Church was amazed that her church is so responsive. She had been working for many months with a family who lived in an apartment house that was about to be condemned. They were the only family remaining in the rather large building. Efforts to place them had failed. Finally the only alternative seemed to be public housing—but there were no apartments for a family of eight. With only a month left, she became desperate and called one of her pastors at eight on Sunday morning. Could an announcement be made asking for help from anyone in the congregation? "I thought it would have to go through the session. You don't even have to take this to a committee. They just announced it!" Two weeks later the family moved into a house rented from a church member. Responsiveness is the key!

In commenting on his style of ministry the pastor of the John Knox Church says:

"We've learned how to be responsive to groups in the community, but also to people within our congregation who see a need and then run with it whether it has to do with resettling a refugee family, starting a counseling center, or developing a food pantry. If people have an idea in the church, even if we aren't sure where it is going, we keep the initiative in the hands of persons concerned and keep involved."

The Pastor as Listener

To be responsive, a pastor must learn to listen. Pastors of ministering congregations are distinguished by their capacity to listen to people. As one parishioner put it: "Our pastor is a good listener. You don't always have pastors who listen. They talk a lot, but don't listen."

The Lay Ministry Questionnaire confirms this difference. Elders of ministering congregations were much more likely than elders in other congregations to say that their pastor listened to people and responded to their needs with caring love. Pastors of ministering congregations agreed with their elders. In contrast to this, pastors in the Presbyterian Panel believed they gave higher priority to listening than did the elders in the Panel.

Perhaps the difference between pastors of ministering congregations and other pastors is in their capacity to demonstrate that they have been listening by responding to what they have heard. The ideas of members are taken seriously and often implemented. Leadership can come from anyone within the congregation. Ideas are sought after. Suggestions consistent with the mission of the Christian church receive support. Help is given to facilitate their implementation. One pastor said, "Even if I don't agree exactly with what they are doing, there are more important things than my approval."

Shaping Program to Gifts

All this illustrates a fundamental stance taken by leaders of ministering congregations. People are more important than programs. The focus is on the gifts they bring to ministry rather than on activities to be staffed by them. The pastor of

Grace Church says, "We recruit for the use of the gifts of people, not for the program of the church."

At first, this emphasis may appear to be in direct contradiction to the earlier assertion that leadership helps stimulate a clear sense of direction and identity in ministering congregations. Actually, each emphasis complements the other. A broad sense of direction, purpose, and identity gives unity and meaning to the different gifts that emerge and the specific thrusts that are encouraged at different points within the fellowship.

Mission groups arise out of the concerns and visions which individuals bring to the congregation. In like fashion, committees and task forces arise out of the life of the congregation.

One reason that the Saint James congregation involved itself in an extensive program of tutoring children of the neighborhood is that the membership of that church includes a large number of active and retired teachers. That resource happened to match the needs of people in the community. The program of the church was responsive to both. The session has consciously sought to structure program in the areas where members of the congregation have abilities. Session members say there is no sense of building a program if you don't have the resources to carry it out.

The Catalytic Function of Leadership

Leaders of ministering congregations see themselves in a catalytic role. They listen, they respond. They also suggest possibilities for service and watch for opportunities to channel interest into active ministry.

Leadership consists of the delicate orchestration of many elements: the needs of the community, a vision of mission, the gifts of individuals and responsiveness to their initiatives. Such responsiveness allows the Spirit of God to move with initiatives even from the most unlikely sources.

An elder of the Green Estates congregation was trying to express to a visitor how the leadership of that congregation functions. He is chairperson of the session committee on social services which carries on an active program in the community.

He told of a sign he once saw on an office wall that expressed their philosophy well. "There they go. I must hasten after them, for I am their leader." His job, he said, "was to learn what is going on, to focus it when possible, and to tap the fantastic reservoir that exists in Green Estates."

The pastor's philosophy of ministry is consistent with that aphorism, but he communicates somewhat better the catalytic quality of his role:

> "I really see myself as a resource. We don't do anything that isn't organically related to the whole. What we do has continuity. It comes out of the resources of our people. My job is to help that happen. It is to help people know who are the other people in the congregation who have the same kinds of concerns, to encourage them to follow the dream, to put it into some kind of actionable form. I see myself as a person who helps people plan what they want to do and to do it."

The pastor of the Garden Hills Church sees himself in a somewhat similar light:

> "The gift I bring is that I am able to build on the ideas of others. I facilitate idea building, spark a group in getting an idea, and motivate them to do something about it."

Both elders and pastors of ministering congregations are much more likely than are other elders and pastors to feel (1) that members of their congregation take the initiative in identifying needs and in proposing ways to serve; (2) that their pastor gives very high priority to responding to the program ideas of others and to helping them implement those ideas; and (3) that members of their congregations have many different ways in which to serve. "Choice is basic to the philosophy of how people develop."

Leaders recognize the wide diversity within the membership of their congregations. Through their responsiveness to all of these divergent interests they open up many different avenues of service that would never develop if programs were left simply to the imagination and resourcefulness of the pastors and sessions of these congregations.

To Choose or Be Chosen?

It is important to make clear that leaders of ministering congregations do not simply wait for initiatives to come from the congregation. They take the initiative in seeking out people who have needed gifts.

More frequently than not, members of these congregations are asked to participate in various programs or acts of ministry. Usually this is a spontaneous process which arises out of the enthusiasm of the people.

Because the major focus is on the use of a member's gifts rather than on filling positions, asking someone to take a particular responsibility actually is being fully responsive to the member. The members are asked to undertake tasks that use their gifts.

In most of the ministering congregations there is a kind of centripetal force that draws new members quickly into the ministries of the congregation. Many new members are active in the life of the congregation long before they unite with the church. Some are so deeply and so contagiously involved as a part of the church family that someone is certain to recruit them for specific projects. It is not unusual for such persons to become deacons, elders, or heads of important committees within the first year or two of membership. This happens only because they have been asked to assume many different responsibilities and have fulfilled them faithfully.

Although opportunities for service are announced, many people do not readily volunteer in response to a general announcement. "After all," an elder in the Pleasant Lake Church said, "there is something about human nature. People like to be asked."

A member of that same church tells of how she got involved in the work of the congregation. "I guess I had filled out one of those white sheets in the Inquirers group. I said I would be interested in helping with arts and crafts or something like that. Without that phone call, I think I would still be sitting at home alone, because I am not the type of person who would just go and jump in myself. I have grown over the past nine years because of the church. They call you and you feel needed. I enjoy doing it."

Often the chairperson of a committee or task force will be responsible for finding people to share in the committee's task and will be assisted by members of the staff or others who know the congregation well. Often the pastor plays a crucial role in approaching people and asking them to serve in ministries that will make use of their experience or their potential.

Identifying Talents

How do leaders of ministering congregations identify the gifts of their members? This skill is obviously crucial in carrying out the style of leadership we have been describing.

To begin with, there is an intuitive quality about the identification of gifts that probably defies description or reproduction. The discerning of gifts is itself a gift. However, that is not the whole story.

Bill Stevens of the Foothill Church clearly is gifted in discerning gifts. One reason for it is the time he spends with members of his congregation. Another is the skill he has developed through training and experience. Bill knows the church family intimately and makes extensive visits in their homes. He interviews new members with a relaxed style that is disarming. He goes into their background and discovers what motivates them or "turns them off." Then, when Bill Stevens presents new members to the session, he shares their background and encourages the new member to do the same. He gets a feel for his flock through shepherding them. He knows them all by name.

Bill Stevens gained many of his skills through professional training as a social worker before he went to seminary. He had learned to interview and had sharpened his capacity to observe and understand people. His natural talent for relating to others has been cultivated rigorously through supervision and extensive experience.

Other pastors, even of large congregations, attest that they are able to identify gifts that people have through their personal contacts with them either in pastoral calling or in small groups. Some of them have set as a number one priority in the first year of a new pastorate getting to know every member of the congregation. The pastor of the Trinity Church took a year and a half to get into every home of the more than three hundred members. He was able to find out the abilities and interests of each member. He made informal notes on individual cards so that he would be able to remind himself of what he had learned. Thus he got a clear idea of what human resources there were in the congregation.

Paul Johnstone, former pastor of the Pleasant Lake Church, was noted for his ability to identify gifts and help people to develop them. How did he do it? The clerk of session replies. "He didn't do it in a vacuum. He would ask my opinion, and he would ask other elders. He was leading many retreats and conferences. He was in small groups a lot. He was getting to know quite a few people. Then if he had someone in mind, he would begin to make contacts and cultivate those contacts. He would work on those people and encourage them. He would have lunch with them, call them up, have them over to his house—all kinds of things."

A new pastor of a church of over two thousand members planned a series of small get-togethers in homes throughout his first year in the parish. His goal was to get to know all the members of that congregation. He too has a gift for relating to people and remembering them personally.

In large congregations, however, it is particularly important to make certain that the task of identifying talents is shared broadly by leaders throughout the congregation. This takes place most frequently in the numerous small groups where people have face-to-face contact on an intimate basis. Leaders of Inquirers groups get to know new members fairly well. They pass on to others information on the particular gifts of each new member. When new members are received, session meetings may be structured so as to give considerable time for each elder to meet with a small group of new members.

The Northern Heights Church has a carefully worked out program for incorporating new members into the life and work of the congregation. Within two weeks of the date when a new member is received, the deacon responsible for his or her parish zone will call in the home with a new-member packet to get acquainted. During that same period a representative of the nominating committee visits new members with a stewardship survey to explore where in the life of the church they would like to serve.

Linking Gifts to Opportunities

Leaders of ministering congregations link members to opportunities for ministry that make effective use of their gifts. They do this informally by suggesting particular avenues of service to individuals, or by giving to the initiator of a service project the names of others who share an interest in that type of service. The leaders may call together several others with common interests or concerns to plan for possible concerted action.

There are of course more formal ways of linking people to possibilities. In some congregations the nominating committee or a service task force functions as a leadership development committee, keeping a list of all the members of the congregation. They seek to discover talents and skills within the congregation, to match those skills to needs for service, and to recommend ways that the church can help its volunteers to be more creative and productive in their ministries.

Human Resources Coordinators

A "human resources coordinator" or a "connector" may be assigned these functions either on a volunteer basis or on a part-time paid basis. Connectors interview new members, keep a record of their interests, and help them find the place of ministry that makes best use of their gifts. In one congregation the human resources coordinator is available to all members by sitting at a table during the family hour following the Sunday morning service once a month. In another congregation different organizations are encouraged to set up tables in the social hall after the service so people can walk about and find more information on possible linkages.

One congregation has employed a part-time staff member to administer its Concern Center. This person must know all the community agencies so that she can refer people in need to sources of help, and channel volunteers to places of service. She administers the congregation's volunteer program to deliver emergency food and clothing to needy families, provide needed transportation with the church's van, and provide emergency housing. Community agencies will come to her when they need volunteers. Members will come to her when they want to get involved in community service. She is the focal point of the congregation's caring ministries both within the congregation and the community.

Some congregations use skills banks. They can be complicated; however, they can be helpful when they are used as a supplement to the more dynamic personal linking. Large congregations have found that a paid staff person may need to take responsibility for operating the skills bank if it is to be kept up to date.

Crisis Support Banks

Both the Trinity Church and the Forest Canyon Church have found a Crisis Support Bank or Grief Bank to be valuable. People who have a personal crisis such as a death in the family, divorce, abortion, alcoholism, or a life-threatening illness or surgery are given an opportunity to "make a desposit" in the Crisis Bank. They sign a sheet on which they check off the areas in which they are willing to share with others. The pastor keeps this in a confidential file. When others face such a crisis, they can make a "withdrawal" from the bank. The pastor puts them in contact with someone who is willing to stand by them in their time of crisis. In the Trinity Church about a hundred out of the 350 members have made deposits. Withdrawals are made about twice a month.

Helping People Discover Their Gifts

Perhaps the best approach to identification, use, and development of gifts is to help people discover their own gifts.

"Teach Gifts" or "Think Gifts" might well be mottoes of many of the ministering congregations. Pastor and session constantly teach members the importance of discovering and developing their own gifts.

In Grace Church when new members have completed the Inquirers group they are encouraged to participate in a series of Discovery groups. In Discovery Group I they search out their spiritual gifts. In Discovery Group II they experiment with using those gifts. From the pulpit and in personal conversation members are continually reminded that they have gifts. They are challenged to discover and make use of them. They are encouraged to tell others about their gifts and then to engage in some ministry that will make use of them. Sometimes this translates rather immediately into a particular form of service. When one member realized that her gifts were in the area of administration she went to the chairperson of the Pastoral Ministries Committee and offered to revise the membership directory, which was badly out of date.

In that congregation, so great an emphasis has been placed upon making use of one's gifts that some members move too quickly from one task to another. A member of the staff who is responsible for recruiting sixty-five church school teachers has been particularly aware of this problem. Members are so stirred emotionally by so many different challenges that every now and then a teacher will ask to be relieved of teaching responsibilities in order to accept another "calling." This staff member insists that teachers complete their one-year commitment to church school teaching. "I don't believe God plays yo-yo," she says.

Another church undertook to educate the whole congregation regarding their gifts. From Easter to Pentecost the ministries committee used the Sunday morning services as an opportunity to highlight gifts for ministry. Using slide presentations and cassette recordings they presented interviews with members of the congregation. Persons were asked to share how they used their gifts for ministry in the office, in the home, and in the community. Each Sunday the sermons were developed on the same theme, alerting people that they do have gifts for ministry and calling them to participate in study groups where they could identify their gifts, develop them, and discover ways to use them in ministry.

Some congregations encourage new members to visit committees or task forces to learn more about what they are doing and to discover whether or not the new members have gifts to offer to the work of a particular group.

Celebrating the Gifts of the People

People discover their own gifts because the pastor and other leaders affirm that they have them. This can begin with the general affirmation which comes with the teaching that all of us are gifted. But it goes beyond that to the specific affirmation of particular gifts. Where gifts are recognized and acknowledged, they will blossom and grow.

Almost everyone appreciates appreciation. Expressing appreciation is an important part of the style of leaders in ministering congregations. Recognition may come informally with a telephone call or in a passing conversation. Saying thank you for jobs well done or identifying a gift that someone has just demonstrated has a multiplying effect. It reinforces the behavior and encourages people to do it again. But it also can become contagious. Those who have been recipients of appreciation are more ready to appreciate someone else.

One pastor believes that the appreciation he expresses to people in his congregation plays a crucial part in encouraging the ministry of the laity. "When someone does something," he says, "I run up and say, 'Hey, that is great.' And then they do more of it." He dictates a continual stream of letters of appreciation. Whenever a parishioner is significantly involved in community service, he sends a note. "You are doing a great job," he writes. "You may not think that what you are doing in the community is related to the church. But you *are* the church in the way you carry on your service. Thank you for your ministry."

Another pastor says: "Affirmation is important. People learn to be open and free with their affirmation of one another. Once it gets rolling, it's like a snowball. It engenders trust, builds a common identity, and is self-perpetuating. Affirmation creates commitment. And that's the fuel that keeps it going."

Some congregations recognize the ministries of particular members by putting a little news article in their church paper. Others may mention such ministries in an occasional Minute for Mission during the morning worship service. Still other congregations have a commissioning service of those who are engaged in community ministries. This demonstrates clearly that the work they are doing in the community is recognized as a ministry by the congregation. Or the congregations may set aside a special Sunday on which to celebrate the ministries of their members.

Supporting the Ministries of the Laity

Affirmation is only one of many ways in which leaders of ministering congregations provide the kind of personal support that will give people the courage to engage in more demanding ministries than they might otherwise be willing to undertake.

The pastor of the John Knox Church is representative of other pastors when he listens to members' concerns, encourages them to use the gifts they have, and gives them confidence to accept the challenge of new ministries. He promises to be with them as they may need his help along the way. And because the people of that congregation trust his judgment and know how well he understands them, the confidence he expresses gives them confidence too. A close pastoral relationship of mutual trust generates the dynamics for helping members to grow at points where they need the courage to try something new or difficult.

The pastor's knowledge of community, government, denominational, and ecumenical resources and his broad contacts with key people enable him to channel materials, speakers, or other resources to members working on important issues. It is little wonder that perhaps 70 percent of the ideas for ministry in the John Knox Church come from lay leaders. Not only does the pastor cultivate the rich resources which they bring, he enables them to tap other valuable resources as well. And his own considerable skills at motivating and organizing are at their service too.

In like manner members of the Foothill congregation will encourage one another by saying: "You can do it! Bill is going to help you." They know that he will stand beside them as mentor and coach when they need him.

Avoiding Burnout

One of the important supportive responsibilities of leaders is to keep people from overextending themselves. This may seem like a strange and welcome dilemma for those whose problem is getting people enthusiastic about anything. But it can be a real problem. Because of the high level of commitment generated in ministering congregations, there is a danger of burnout. People are so enthusiastic, so deeply involved, and so broadly committed that they wear themselves out and withdraw. To minimize the possibility of burnout, leaders of ministering congregations encourage persons to be selective in the tasks they accept and to recognize the importance of pacing their service. Certain leaders will drop out of active leadership for a time. They continue as part of the fellowship and usually return to active leadership after a period of months or years.

For some individuals there appears to be a certain rhythm of involvement. For one period they may be very active within the internal ministries of the congregation. Subsequently, they may be more active in community-based ministries or may drop out of service activities for a while. Volunteer service often develops employable skills. So one member who has spent large amounts of time as a volunteer may later find that the skills acquired have led to employment.

A Series of Small Achievable Steps

Leaders of ministering congregations cultivate the gifts of members through a series of small achievable steps. As each small step of ministry has been successfully taken, subsequent, more difficult, steps become achievable. Small increments of successful ministry open the way to deeper and broader involvement in ministry.

In describing how they became committed in the ministries of their congregation, members speak of the way in which they moved rather quickly from one level of involvement to another. Members may read Scripture in a church school class, then lead in prayer. Reading Scripture or giving the call to worship in the Sunday morning worship service may be next. Then they may help plan a worship service or serve on a worship task force. From this they may go on to serve as deacons and then as elders.

Looking back to a former pastorate, members of the congregation in the Pleasant Lake Church speak of that pastor's gift for sensing what people might be able to do and getting them to do it at a pace at which they would grow and develop. "We had an informal process at work in the church whereby people were given responsibilities. As they executed them in a way that seemed reasonable, they moved on to greater responsibilities. The thing just kept snowballing. I think that Paul was carefully watching certain people, so that he sensed when it was the right time for them to take on more responsibility."

Opportunities for service are offered in small packages. People are asked to commit themselves to particular responsibilities for limited and specific periods of time. As one volunteer said, "Programs are definite and easy to respond to." The pastor of Old First Church feels this is important.

> "We use task forces instead of committees that tie people down forever. Because it's a short period, people will serve. And in the end, once they start serving, sometimes they continue to serve."

Bill Stevens of the Foothill Church is a good illustration. His parishioners see him as a teacher.

> "He breaks things down for you as much as you need, as often as you need for your own growth. He makes you feel able to function in the area you are dealing with."

Small incremental steps of successful achievement are effective in drawing people into deeper and deeper involvement. Some may joke about "getting trapped." "You start coming to meetings. Then, well, it's your turn to help prepare the meeting for the next time. The next thing you know you're holding office. Soon you hear that presbytery needs officers too." And so it goes.

Do It Your Way

"I think you can do it," said the pastor of the John Knox Church. "You can use your own style." Here is an important clue to the development of the gifts that members bring to ministry. If they are to be highly motivated to use their gifts in ministry, they must be free to do things their way.

To let members develop ideas in their own way takes a special kind of leadership. Many able persons who have achieved positions of responsibility are highly skilled in doing things themselves. Having achieved nominal leadership, they are inclined to feel that they know best how things should be done. Unfortunately, pastors are not immune from this human tendency. It is not easy to trust others enough to let them do it *their* way. It is even more difficult to give members the kind of coaching they need for their growth and increased effectiveness without making them feel you are directing them to do it *your* way.

As one parishioner puts it, she has hesitated to present her ideas to some pastors because they have given her the feeling that they would be judgmental. "Being so good," she says, "they would take over." Another says, "A good leader is best if, when objectives are fulfilled, people will say, 'We did this ourselves.'"

Psychological Success

A helpful theoretical framework for understanding the dynamics of ministering congregations is Kurt Lewin's concept of psychological success. He has shown that people will feel successful in a working situation (1) when they choose their own goals; (2) when their goals are felt to be challenging and meaningfully related both to their self-concept and to the goals of the organization; (3) when the means of reaching them have been self-determined; and (4) when the goals are achieved.[20]

All of these elements are present in the style of leadership exercised in ministering congregations. We have seen that the importance of choice is emphasized as people determine what ministries they will undertake. Members are encouraged to understand their own gifts and to make use of those gifts in their ministries. They exercise their ministries in relation to and within the context of a congregation that has a clear sense of mission. They are allowed the freedom to do it their way. And they are asked to undertake tasks that are achievable, but they are challenged to grow toward the complete realization of their potential. An elder from the Forest Canyon Church puts this all in his own words when he says:

> "I think the leadership that we have has produced a climate where people can experience success in a very vital kind of human way. Most people tend to hold back and to underestimate their own potentials. They are afraid to venture forth. I think that this community is a very safe place. And once you are successful, then you feel better about yourself. Then you have invested some of what you are in this place. It's a part of you then. And when we all have created something that is a part of ourselves, then we all own it and share it, and it becomes an extension of ourselves. That's the whole dynamic of community."

Partnership in ministry facilitates that sense of community. Pastors work as colleagues of other church leaders and of members of the congregation. Each may have different functions and different gifts and different training. But there is one Spirit that binds them together. Neither the pastor nor the session can allow themselves to be put on a pedestal because they are thought to have superior knowledge or authority or power. They must provide the leadership and the resources that the congregation needs. But that leadership must be that of a servant. For it is still true today that "the servant is not greater than his lord." How can servant leadership be exercised? That is the subject of Chapter 7.

CHAPTER 7

Sharing Power as Partners

He who is greatest among you shall be your
servant.
(Matt. 23:11)

The great leader is seen as servant first, and
that simple fact is the key to his greatness.
(Robert Greenleaf, *Servant Leadership*)[21]

The big remaining issue is that of power. The power that
pastors and elders wield can either thwart or free the people
of God to exercise their ministries. When power is used within
the church to protect position, status, or privilege within hierarchical structures it will kill shared ministry within the congregation. If it is true, as has been suggested, that the ministry
of members to one another is the training ground for ministry
to others outside the intimate Christian community, then such
exercise of power will ultimately dampen the ardor of members in carrying out their ministries in the world. On the other
hand, power that is shared freely and openly for the building
up of the body of Christ can be liberating and stimulating to
the ministry of the people of God in the world.

The offices of pastor and elder exist to enable the ministries
of all the people of God. They carry with them certain responsibilities for the governing of the church. This combination of
functions creates both opportunities and pitfalls.

Letty Russell, in her book *The Future of Partnership*, suggests the leadership ideal:

Christian community is *koinōnia:* a partnership of discipleship modeled on servanthood and not on hierarchical structures of domination

131

and subordination (John 13:1–17). Its strength and power come from the power of self-actualization for others, not from selfishness. Leadership gifts that emerge are functional and not for status. . . .

In Christian communities leadership behavior that is shared among various persons for the purpose of service may become a gift that is multiplied by the one whose Spirit makes service possible.[22]

Pastors of ministering congregations have a high commitment to shared ministry. They have a readily articulated philosophy and theology of ministry based upon Biblical and theological convictions which affirm that ministry is the work of all the people. These things have already been made clear. It now remains to describe, in quite specific terms, how their convictions are translated into reality. To begin with, these pastors are willing to pay a high price, if necessary, to achieve partnership. Along the way they may have had to struggle with themselves, with their sessions, and even with the membership of their congregations to clarify what this means. In partnership with their sessions they have discovered how to organize the work of ministry and make partnership possible.

Pastors of ministering congregations are more than twice as likely as other pastors to feel very strongly that they share leadership as genuine partners with lay leaders. They say that frequently they have observed pastors and lay persons seeking a relationship in which there is freedom to complement each other's knowledge and skills. Elders of these congregations concur in their pastor's judgments.

The Power Struggle

John C. Harris comments in *Stress, Power and Ministry* on the feeling of powerlessness of many clergy in our day. They face high levels of role ambiguity, role confusion, and role conflict with their congregations.

The sense of powerlessness which they share with lay leaders arises because they cannot decide how role conflicts are to be resolved. The authority of the pastoral office has eroded. This is part of a general redistribution of power in society as a whole and of movements toward more participatory democracy. It has resulted in a "growing insistence of laity that the pastor's power is everybody's business. . . . We are divided and unclear about how to resolve conflicts between clergy and laity. We are divided about the use of power."[23]

If the issue of power is as crucial as Harris suggests, and there is much evidence that he is right, then the discovery of ways to share power and make partnership come alive in a congregation has great significance for the church in our time. In sharp contrast to the feelings of powerlessness and confusion that many pastors have is the sense of liberation, purposefulness, and accomplishment that pastors of ministering congregations display. They have discovered creative ways to share power. Through collaboration they have released the potential of those who work with them as well as their own.

The Pedestal Phenomenon

Pedestals are a problem. Although the pastor's authority has eroded, a considerable aura of mystery and respect for the pastoral office remains. This is particularly true among the older and more active members of traditional congregations. For many, the pastor is still on a pedestal. The pastor is a member of a profession whose members are highly educated. And in an age of specialization, professionals are given a great deal of deference in their particular fields.

The preacher interprets the word of God from a pulpit which is lifted up above the people. This reinforces any tendencies to rely on one-way communication. Preachers are selected for their ability to talk rather than to listen. And one of the decisive moments in the selection of a new pastor is when the *Pulpit* Nominating Committee, as many still call it, listens to the candidate's sermon. Many people who seek help from a pastor are seeking certainty in the midst of uncertainty. They want to be told what to do. The temptation to give them what they want is very great.

The pedestal phenomenon is deeply rooted. The role models of many who have gone into the professional ministry were authoritarian persons who commanded a great deal of respect and wielded considerable influence within the congregation. For generations, it has been commonly assumed that the pastor should somehow be a model of Christian perfection and thus be something more than human. For both pastor and people a gulf must be bridged if they are really to be on a par.

Finally the pastoral office is clothed with a certain amount of ecclesiastical power. Pastors are "set apart" by ordination. This gives them the right to do things that others are not permitted to do. They administer the Sacraments, perform weddings, and in the Presbyterian tradition have ultimate authority over what they preach. Even in a form of government where parity of pastors and elders is emphasized, as in the Reformed tradition, parity is weakened because ordained ministers are the only continuing members of presbytery. Furthermore, it is very difficult indeed to make partnership a living reality when one partner is paid to give full attention to the task and the other must be content to give only part-time attention to it. Elders may come and go, but pastors are not easily removed from office if they do not choose to go. They have ecclesiastical power.

Climbing Down off the Pedestal

If partnership in ministry is to occur in any congregation, ways must be found to get the pastor down off the pedestal. Pastors themselves have an important part to play. They must want to come down. Pastors of ministering congregations have made that decision unequivocally. Frequently it has been a struggle for them. Emotionally they may be inclined to be pulpit stars or otherwise to accept the traditional elevated status of being a "member of the cloth." But they have found ways to deal with themselves and their personal needs.

The natural gifts of some make partnership particularly difficult for them. The pastor of one large ministering congregation tells of the price he has had to pay to move in that direction.

"I was ready for a change in the pattern of my ministry from being the superstar minister to being in a collegial style of ministry.

"I became committed to *vigorous fellowship,* which includes the kind of confrontation among the staff members that makes us open to being 'pruned.' I told our staff that was my goal and they agreed. Pruning was a painful process. I have learned not simply to try to sell my dreams. I am a natural salesman and I've learned to pull back. That is not my natural style, for I always have been the quarterback or the captain of the team. I have the gift of igniting and uniting."

This pastor is still a natural salesman. He continues to use his gift for igniting and uniting. But together with his colleagues he is shaping those gifts and is using them within a collegial framework. Another member presides at staff meetings. They make decisions by concensus. And continue to *prune* one another.

The Need for High Levels of Personal Security

It is a risky business to come down off the pedestal. Pastors become vulnerable because they are no longer in a protected role. They must make it on their own. A truly shared ministry requires a high level of personal security in pastors. They must not be threatened by strong lay leaders. They must yield the need to control, and be involved in everything that goes on in the congregation.

One pastor tells his own story this way:

"It took a long time for me to give up my controlling and my defensiveness. Now openness characterizes my leadership. Yet I do not hesitate to take strong leadership to press for decisions I feel are important.

"I have learned to trust that God's Spirit is at work in other styles and theologies—wherever faithful people gather. I appreciate what others have to say. I listen more and have given up being so right. When I did this I saw how things shifted. The Holy Spirit did new and innovative things."

Two Things Are Necessary

To develop a genuine partnership in ministry two things are essential. First of all, it is important for pastors to have support from others who share their goal. The temptations to get back on the pedestal are strong and subtle. Without support, leaders can easily yield to the pressure to do the work themselves rather than helping people to do it. As early as possible in a pastoral relationship the session itself should become the pastor's colleague in developing true partnership. A small personnel committee made up of sensitive and supportive persons may become an important support group. The chairperson of such a personnel committee said of its relationship to its pastors, "We pick them up, brush them off, and send them back into the fray."

Secondly, pastors must have a positive dream of what partnership in ministry can mean. Without such a dream, climbing down off the pedestal is essentially a negative endeavor. One is seeking to *give up* position and power. Why give up attractive benefits unless there are rewards to replace them? What is it that we are seeking when we come down off the pedestal? It is the fulfillment which one experiences when a congregation comes alive. It is the deep satisfaction one discovers in the maturing of others. It is the joy of sharing power, and the freedom which such sharing brings. One pastor speaks for others when he says: "Somewhere along the line I have gotten in my bones that giving away power is fun! So I don't really feel any great sacrifice or any ego threat in doing that. It may be that certain ministers in certain situations would be afraid to give power, or something. But I think that if they only knew what a load they would get off their backs, they would do it."

The Servant Leader

The positive alternative to the pedestal style of leadership is servant leadership. It is leadership such as that of the One who came as Suffering Servant and gave his life that the world may have life. This kind of leadership serves the highest priority needs of others and prizes the valuable contribution each individual makes to the whole.

Robert Greenleaf, in his book *Servant Leadership,* recounts the story from Hermann Hesse's *The Journey to the East* in which a band of men on a mythical journey are accompanied by a servant named Leo. Leo "does their menial chores, but ... also sustains them with his spirit and his song. He is a person of extraordinary presence. All goes well until Leo disappears. Then the group falls into disarray and the journey is abandoned. They cannot make it without the servant Leo." Years later a member of the party becomes a member of the order that sponsored the journey. Only then does he discover that Leo, the servant, is in reality "the titular head of the Order, its guiding spirit, a great and noble *leader.*"[24]

In Greenleaf's paradigm the Servant-Leader is servant first and leader second, making certain that the most important needs of others are being served. Others may aspire to leadership out of a drive for power or possessions. They are leaders first. Greenleaf believes that society is moving toward the acceptance of servant leadership.

Whether or not one can accept Greenleaf's vision of the future, his picture of the servant leader is thoroughly Christian in its underlying philosophy and remarkably congruent with leadership styles in ministering congregations.

It is what Harris describes in his discussion of collaboration when he says: "From this perspective, the pastor is seen, not as *the* sacramental person, but as one sacramental presence among many in a rich, differentiated expression of functions, talents, individuals and tasks in the congregation's life. Pastors are learning to see that having influence does not mean calling all the shots."[25]

The Corporate Struggle

Climbing down off the pedestal can be painful. The early days of transition from a pastor-centered ministry to a shared ministry often involve a rigorous corporate struggle with deeply entrenched expectations. Elders, deacons, and church members must buy into the vision of partnership in ministry. The inertia of long years of past practice must be overcome.

The Pleasant Lake congregation had long been a respectable traditional congregation. Many years ago the members called to their pulpit a brilliant preacher. Those who remember him still say, "He was the greatest preacher I have ever heard—just eloquent." The new preacher filled the sanctuary. They opened up the Sunday school, and he filled that. So they built a huge new sanctuary and educational plant in the center of a growing residential area of town.

During the ten years of that preaching ministry the membership of the congregation more than doubled, from perhaps five hundred to well over twelve hundred. When the time came to seek a new pastor, the congregation again sought someone who could preach with power. But they were looking for something more. They were ready for change. The new pastor was an excellent preacher. But he also brought with him a new strategy which people now feel made possible the renewal they have experienced. "He changed our church from a monologue situation to a dialogue situation." Before he came, people had little opportunity to participate beyond the worship service. He introduced the concept of Koinonia groups. In those groups people could raise questions they never had a chance to ask before. They were involved in dialogue about Jesus Christ. There were retreats and special conferences. A nucleus of about fifty to one hundred persons (out of 1,500) were deeply involved. They began to discover a completely new dimension to their faith.

> "In the retreats and in his conferences, as soon as people knew a little they were in leadership roles so that you were having to lead a discussion before you even knew what the discussion was about. He was making you grow up in the experience. We had some wonderful experiences. And we would see people that we knew and loved offering their lives to Jesus Christ for the first time."

The first step in the new pastor's strategy was to work with the session. He spent time with them. There were session retreats. He worked with them as a Koinonia group. He got them to *be* the session. They set up planning task forces and established goals for the work of the congregation. They moved younger persons into places of leadership and put people to work. The session established a joint budget committee with the trustees. Only then did they gain control of setting priorities. "From that point on things began to grow and the session actually began to assume its proper responsibilities under the *Book of Order.*"

There were many failures. People opposed change. The new young pastor had to "step into a pulpit with the greatest preacher in America and compete. And a lot of people did not want to transfer their loyalty. There was a lot of resistance. It was a tremendously traumatic period, and he nearly failed." The struggle for partnership in ministry was so intense that the pastor almost resigned in despair.

Toward a Strategy for Change

In examining this case study of change from a traditional congregation to a ministering congregation, several things stand out as clues for developing a strategy for such changes.

1. *A clear strategy was broadly accepted.* This began with the new pastor. But quickly he secured ownership from the session and other leaders of the congregation.

2. *Initially, the pastor concentrated on a few key people.* He worked with the session, knowing that decision makers must be at the center of any change that has a lasting effect. Collegiality that does not involve both pastor and lay leaders is not collegiality at all.

The pastor identified other key people with leadership potential and involved them in Koinonia groups, retreats, and other development activities.

Pastors of ministering congregations know that they can have a deep and influential relationship with only a few people. Therefore, their strategies focus on those individuals who have the greatest possibility of becoming multipliers.

3. *He worked to change entrenched expectations* about the life and work of the congregation and about his role. Traditional assumptions about a pulpit-centered ministry had been reinforced by a highly successful preacher. These had to change.

4. *He modeled collegiality in ever-widening circles of renewal, influence, and power.* He started with a core group. Anyone who began to buy into the dream was asked to take leadership responsibilities. This involved them in collegiality from the start, and gave them ownership. Soon it involved others beyond the core group.

5. *After a period of great stress enough leaders emerged to make possible a turning point.* Initially, the outcome was in doubt. Despair always seemed just around the corner. Change was slow and painful. Then came enough change in the session and in the congregational leadership that more change became possible. A tipping point had been reached. The level of lay involvement became sufficiently high to change the dynamics of the congregation. When that "critical mass" of lay involvement was reached, lay ministry became contagious. Increasing numbers of members served as models of lay ministry. Support of their common ministries became a normal part of the fellowship. The congregation got a reputation which attracted others of like mind. A new congregational identity emerged making shared ministry a reality.

Congregations with high rates of turnover in membership can hasten the time when the tipping point comes by concentrating on inducting new members. In fact, without it, they may never reach the goal. Too many uncommitted and uninvolved members will dilute the total mixture as one by one committed leaders leave.

Changing Members' Perceptions

The first and most difficult task is to help church members change their understanding of the pastor's role. One pastor observed:

"My experience tells me that it is *extremely important for pastors to help church members conceptualize shared ministry.* For many Presbyterians these days, their cultural experience runs counter to any idea of shared ministry. That is, they tend to function in a business or professional world where specialization is the order of the day and where decisions, made by a few, are to be carried out by many. They enter the church with a mind-set that says, 'It is the job of the hired help (i.e., the pastors) to do the work of ministry.' Pastors, therefore, have to work diligently with new members, with session, trustees, deacons, committees, etc., to teach about shared ministry. Much preaching and teaching needs to be done. Our people need to get in touch with the theological and Biblical underpinnings for the idea of shared ministry."

The enormity of the task is emphasized by one of the most important findings of this study. There is a high level of *agreement* between pastors and elders in ministering congregations on expectations regarding the work of the church and partnership in ministry. In contrast, there is a high level of *disagreement* between pastors and elders in other congregations on these matters. (See Appendix 3.)

The differences are startling. Pastors and elders in the Presbyterian Panel disagreed with one another in a high proportion of their answers to the Lay Ministry Questionnaire.

This was particularly true on the 28 questions which best summarize the themes of this book. Fourteen questions describe the priorities that pastors give to styles of leadership, and fourteen other questions describe the ways that congregations live and work together. On those 28 items pastors and elders of the ministering congregations disagreed with one another on only five items (18 percent). Pastors and elders in the Presbyterian Panel disagreed on twenty-two (79 percent).

It is obvious that in ministering congregations there is a *high level* of agreement between pastors and elders on what the church is all about and on the nature of partnership. In other Presbyterian congregations there is a *low level* of agreement about these things.

Role Conflicts and What to Do About Them

This confirms what many already know: that there are significant role conflict problems that pastors and sessions must deal with. A role conflict exists when there are two differing sets of expectations which push a person in distinctly different directions. Often the differences are mutually exclusive. Role ambiguities exist when mutual expectations are unclear to the people involved. Role conflicts and ambiguities are debilitating. They interfere with a pastor's effectiveness and with the effectiveness of the session.

There are many different ways to reduce role conflict and ambiguity.[26] One way is to make the conflict visible to all parties involved. Ministering congregations have developed high levels of mutual understanding about partnership in ministry and the role and style of the pastor, because they are *communicating* with one another about these things. They work on the issues involved.

It is important to clarify mutual expectations between pastors, elders, and members. This may be done quite informally. When the pastor of the Trinity Church began his work he invited the session to schedule a time to share their expectations of one another. They liked the idea and set aside an evening to do so. Each member of the session came prepared for the discussion by writing down three things expected of the pastor. The pastor shared his expectations. Out of the resulting conversation emerged three or four priorities for his time during the first year. Thus was laid a solid foundation for partnership.

There are many different ways to clarify expectations. The Pastoral Expectations Inventory, developed by the Vocation Agency of the United Presbyterian Church,[27] makes use of a listing of twenty-four different activities in which pastors are often involved. The Pastoral Activities Index,[28] from which the list was derived, fairly represents the kinds of things pastors are most often expected to do. Participants in the clarification process are asked to indicate the relative priority of each activity for the total work of the congregation. In like manner they make individual judgments as to the priorities each activity ought to have in the pastor's work. (See Appendix 4.) They then arrive at a consensus on the priorities which each activity should have in the life of their congregation and in the work of the pastor. This process often leads to the conclusion that certain high priority activities should not be carried out by the pastor but should instead be the work of the elders, deacons, or other groups within the life of the congregation. The process also calls for making reasonable estimates about the amount of time which a pastor needs to spend on each type of activity. This usually leads to the realization that too much is being expected of the pastor. Adjustments are then made to reach a consensus on a reasonable work load. The group then decides on who should pick up responsibilities which the pastor must drop.

Still another way of dealing with expectations focuses less on activities as such and deals more specifically with pastoral style. The Ministry Survey (Appendix 1) makes use of forty-two items from the Lay Ministry Questionnaire. These are the questions that most readily distinguish between ministering congregations and other congregations in their leadership styles and understandings of ministry.

Pastor and session can independently answer these forty-two questions. Then in comparing their answers they will have the stimulus for dialogue on ways to move more actively toward partnership in ministry.

Clarity of the Pastor's Own Role Understanding

Pastors of ministering congregations have clear role expectations for themselves and their people. They know who they are, what their strengths and limitations are, and what contribution they can best make to the whole. Such self-understanding provides the basis for a greater sense of professional security and for more productive dialogue with members of session. Pastors of ministering congregations are much more likely than other pastors to feel that they have a clear sense of their own appropriate roles in relation to the roles of church officers and members. Elders agree with them.

Modeling Collegiality

It is most important to clarify role expectations. But it is even more important to demonstrate genuine partnership in the quality of collegial relationships which a pastor has with other staff and with lay leaders of the congregation. Where there is more than one pastor, it is crucial that they model partnership in the way they work together. The pastor of one congregation says: "Our staff models the kind of Christian community we are inviting others to experience. We are close to each other and think of each other as brothers and sisters, which has been a wonderful experience for all of us."

In like manner, pastor and elders must discover and demonstrate what shared leadership is like. If it doesn't happen in the session, it will never happen in the congregation. As pastors model collegiality with one another, with the staff, and with the session, elders are encouraged to develop collegial relationships with members of the committees with which they work. Committee members in turn will become partners in ministry with other members of the congregation. It is like ripples in a pond. Here is a staff member of Grace Church. What is her task? we ask. "My job is to disciple the members of the base group," she replies. And what is discipling? It is "giving people the enthusiasm, courage, and equipment to grow and minister within the body of Christ." Another staff member says, "The pastor models ministry to us and we model it to others."

Another pastor is much in demand outside the congregation to lead renewal retreats. He refuses to accept such engagements unless one or more lay leader colleagues are a part of the team. Evangelism teams make use of an apprentice approach. Each teacher of a Bible class chooses someone from the group as a helper in leading the group. New teachers are always in the making.

Delegating and Communicating

Closely related to collegiality is the capacity to assign responsibilities to different members of a team and let each follow through completely with his or her own part of the whole task. This is not as easy as one may be tempted to think. Loss of control is a threat to a conscientious leader who wants to make certain that everything goes well in the church and its program. It is easier to do things yourself. One is likely either to overcontrol or to abdicate responsibility. The middle ground is difficult. Pastors of ministering congregations are convinced that it is neither feasible nor desirable to do everything themselves. The risk must be taken. So these pastors would join in saying: "In a ministry like this you have to be willing not to have your hand in everything. Some pastors would find that hard. Sometimes you don't know what is going on. And sometimes you wish you didn't."

Benign Neglect

Failure can sometimes be redemptive and lead to higher levels of responsibility. But it takes courage and discriminating judgment to know when to let something fall apart because the person responsible for doing it has not taken responsibility seriously. Because the pastors of ministering congregations have a clear vision of the crucial importance of lay leadership, they are willing to let some things fail, if necessary, in order to ensure that the laity takes seriously its share of ministry. This practice says to the person involved: "Your part of the task is crucial to all of us. We cannot do without you."

Pastors learn to sense when a little "benign neglect," as one of them calls it, can be productive rather than destructive of shared leadership. They have discovered that there are times and situations when failing to play the rescue game can lead to the strengthening of the fiber of mutual responsibility.

"We were supposed to have a little reception after church this Sunday after our congregational meeting," one pastor reported. "The laity that were supposed to get it together didn't do it. So it didn't happen."

Another pastor echoed this strategy. "I allow some things to drop through the cracks, just as a way of saying: 'That dropped through the cracks because you weren't functioning there. Another time it shouldn't fail if you function properly.' It's been a good teaching tool." In commenting on that pastor's style, one of the members said, "He gives people responsibility and authority and allows them to make a mistake." Indeed it is a good teaching tool when used judiciously and supportively!

Structuring for Partnership in Ministry

We have been exploring ways in which leaders work with people to draw out the best in them. Many of these are person-to-person skills which most leaders can cultivate. Now, it is important to look beyond such questions of personal style to the issue of creating structures that make shared ministry possible. How do pastors and lay leaders work together to develop structures and processes that will facilitate partnership? Who makes decisions and how? How wide is the involvement in planning within the congregation? How difficult is it for a member of the congregation to take the initiative and generate a new idea that bears fruit in a program of the congregation? Where do ideas come from and who implements them?

Conflict Between Movements and Institutional Structures

There is a classic conflict between movements and institutional structures. Movements arise in response to charismatic leadership with powerful dreams that call for innovation. They may arise out of the failures of older structures. Institutional structures often are the product of former movements that have been organized to ensure continuity, coherence, and conformity. They may persist even when the soul of the former movement has been lost altogether. They may lose their capacity to change.

In various epochs of the church's history this pattern has repeated itself—from movement to structure. From the priestly to the prophetic. From the upper room to the Constantian church. From the monastic movement to the oppressive legalisms of the Middle Ages. From the Reformation vision to well-established denominations. From sects to churches. From frontier revivals to comfortable congregations. From the early missionary movement to mission boards and indigenous churches.

Someone has asked, "Can the church be trusted with mission?" Is not mission a movement rather than an institution? Is not ecclesiastical structure sure to kill the ministry of the laity?

Movements Can Thrive Within Church Structures

It is possible to structure the church so as to encourage movements of ministry within ecclesiastical structures. It is possible to combine order and ardor. It is not easy, but it can be done. And ministering congregations are showing us the way. Ministering congregations encourage a wide variety of things to happen without everyone having to be involved. They legitimize opportunities for some to undertake activities which the decision makers themselves would not undertake. Within agreed upon limits there is room for a great deal of diversity. Leaders avoid imposing unnecessary limitations on the program possibilities that can emerge from members of the congregation.

Defensive Structuring

Pastors of ministering congregations structure the work of the session and of the staff, if any, to curb any tendencies they may have to dominate those groups. One pastor has asked the session to schedule its commissions to meet simultaneously so he cannot possibly be present in all of them as they do their work. He knows that committees will ask his opinion and he will give it. He tends to dominate discussions and generates too high a proportion of the ideas. So he floats from one commission to another.

Structuring for Collegiality

The pastor of the Forest Canyon Church has developed a collegial team of part-time specialists. He carries the basic administrative and coordinative responsibilities, but the specialists are free to work in their own areas with their own committees. "They don't have to run and find me and get my approval. In their specialities they are more gifted than I am. They bring those specialities and we work as a team. We have a lot of phone contact—just clearing signals, getting some kind of report back. We may bounce things off one another, but they don't have to get approval by me."

The Pedestal of Power on Which the Session Sits

If ministry is to arise out of the life of the congregation, the session must share its decision-making powers. Like the pastor, the session also sits on a pedestal. Out of all members in a congregation a few are elected to guide its spiritual life and welfare. They are the decision makers. And as one pastor puts it, "they get their kicks out of saying yes or no." They are in a power position. In many Presbyterian congregations everything must wait for a decision by the session. Any change in the program, any new or innovative ideas, any plans to involve persons in ministry are first approved by the session. The Constitution of the denomination gives them great power and responsibility. The congregation as a whole elects the pastor, approves the budget, chooses elders and deacons, and hears annual reports. But the decisions on admitting or dismissing new members and on the programs of the church are all made by the session.

Years ago, before coming to the Forest Canyon Church, their pastor Tom became convinced that this concentration of power in one body was stultifying to the growth of members and their ministries. Early in his ministry Tom had served as an assistant pastor under an authoritarian pastor who insisted on approving everything that was done in the church. "It became a vast extension of his ego," Tom says, "and I just decided that I didn't want to be in a church like that. I learned more from that negative model than I did from, say, a positive model. It got me emotionally. It got past my head."

Tom began to think about the ministry of all the people of God. A seminar in a nearby university introduced him to the idea of vertical and horizontal models of administration. Personally, he had experienced the devastating frustration of the hierarchical model and was ready to try the horizontal model.

He had experienced the terrible waste of committees who have no authority to do anything but talk and make reports. He tells of a community action committee in a church he served in the early '60s! They spent an entire evening trying to plan a race relations panel discussion, only to decide that the session would probably not approve it because some elders were anxious about race relations. He saw initiative and creativity suppressed at that point. "What the session needs," he concluded, "is to exercise a real level of trust in the people who are members of the congregation." And so a new approach was generated.

The Session Gives Away Authority

When Tom came to the Forest Canyon Church he estimated that 20 percent of the people in the congregation were doing 80 percent of the work. Today 80 percent of the people are deeply involved in the life of the congregation. There has been a dramatic shift in levels of involvement. This came in relationship to a similar dramatic shift of power.

When Tom arrived, the session was divided. Membership had dropped from 750 to 450. The session was ready for almost anything. When Tom proposed that they give away the power to act without giving away their ultimate responsibility for those actions they were willing to consider it. They agreed that as a session they had been elected by the family of the church to "bear ultimate responsibility and therefore to have ultimate authority for the health and welfare of the family." They could not give away their ultimate responsibility, but they could delegate authority. They would take a big risk. They would give people the authority to exercise certain ministries. They would trust them as responsible adults to care about the church's life and to act responsibly in areas for which they were given authority.

Within carefully specified policy guidelines and budget limitations each committee is free to act on programs without reference back to session. The pastor meets with most of the major committees and spends considerable time working with chairpersons of each committee. A member of session sits with each committee to maintain close liaison with what is being done. But decisions are made by each committee.

For example, the community action committee may speak and act in its own name. It can announce that it has taken a position on a particular issue. It can endorse candidates through the church newsletter and put things in the newspaper. It cannot do *direct* advocacy of its position during worship on Sunday morning. But it can do *indirect* advocacy by announcing its position and inviting people who want to talk about it to meet with them during the family hour after the service. In that context the committee can explain why it has taken a particular position, argue for it, and encourage people to support it. The committee cannot speak for the whole church, nor do all church members agree with everything every committee does, but the committees are allowed freedom within limits to act as responsible units of the church.

Every member of the session has the right at any session meeting to raise a concern about the work of any of the committees. If the session decides that serious issues are at stake in a committee's program which may not have been taken into account by that committee, the session asks for an opportunity to dialogue with that committee. A representative of the session may meet with the chairperson of the committee. The committee may then decide to change its course of action or may insist upon doing what it had planned. In the latter case, the session must then decide whether it is willing to let the committee proceed or whether the consequences of that course of action are so far-reaching that the session must shut down the committee and get another one. That is the session's ultimate authority. So far, the session has not had to exercise it.

Each year all committees review their authority delegation descriptions and propose possible changes to the session. In that process the session can enlarge, narrow, or modify the range of authority it has given to any particular committee.

The Forest Canyon Church is enthusiastic about the way it has organized its life and work. The pastor is convinced that its structure is one of the most important keys to the high levels of involvement of members in the ministries of that congregation. Certainly it seems to have released a great deal of creativity and energy.

Critical elements in the success of this approach are: (1) the

clarity of the authority delegation descriptions, (2) the maintenance of high levels of communication between the session
and its committees, and (3) the pastor's own deep involvement
in the work of the major committees. The pastor and elder
representative of session who meet with each committee have
early opportunities to make their particular contributions
where needed and can sense any potential problems before
they grow out of proportion.

How Other Sessions Do It

In Grace Church base groups are given considerable autonomy in developing their particular areas of ministry. They are
guided by the covenants they have made which have already
been approved by session. Several of the base group leaders
were heard to say, in relation to the program of their base
group, "The buck stops here."

In other congregations the session establishes departments
or commissions to which they delegate considerable responsibility for making programmatic decisions. Usually such commissions operate in connection with a churchwide planning
process that gets broad involvement of every member. In
large congregations with complex programs there may be
quite a number of large departments. Each of them will be
subdivided into specific "ministries." Functions to be carried
out take priority over reports to be made by subcommittees.

In very small congregations there may be a minimum of
committee structure. Much of the work is done through ad hoc
groups. This way of working may actually provide an ideal
context for encouraging program to arise out of the initiatives
of members.

Participative Planning

Whatever the structural arrangements within a congregation, the underlying principle is to discover ways to get broad
involvement in planning and carrying out the work of the
congregation. When each elder on the session chairs a depart-

ment and recruits five or six other persons to carry specific responsibilities within that functional area, involvement of members has been multiplied five or six fold. When each individual department member recruits other individuals to help develop and carry out particular programs, the involvement of the whole congregation increases by geometrical proportion.

Most ministering congregations have effective planning processes which give opportunities for such broad involvement of officers and of the membership as a whole.

The John Knox Church is part of a consortium of four congregations who do much of their programming together. Each year, on the weekend after Labor Day, as many as 250 persons from the four congregations gather at a conference grounds on a nearby lake. All members are invited, though there is a worship service back home for the remnant that do not go. There are inspirational speakers, Bible studies, and various planning activities which set directions for the joint ministries of those congregations during the coming year.

In many congregations, planning retreats play an important role in setting directions. The 116-member Saint John's congregation invites members to an overnight planning retreat. Opportunity is provided for brainstorming. Everyone participates in generating ideas. Out of the discussion priorities emerge and are agreed upon. The pastor observes that "if you come out of that with an action plan, something usually happens. Otherwise you are lost."

Many larger churches involve all officers in their planning retreats but use other mechanisms for getting suggestions from members. When departments and their committees have organized to include a broad cross section of the congregation, much of the preliminary work on direction-setting may draw upon ideas generated by church members in those committees. Officers then meet to shape proposals which ultimately are approved by the session. When the session has established the major outlines of the program, then departments, commissions, or committees do the more detailed planning of specific programs.

Whatever the method, participative planning is an essential

ingredient in the development of a ministering congregation. If programs are planned by the pastor and "sold" to the session, without their significant involvement, partnership is greatly hampered. Participative planning is more time-consuming. It may seem easier for the pastor to do it himself. But in the long run that only increases the burden the pastor must carry because it is being carried alone or in the face of subtle foot-dragging or even less subtle opposition.

Ministering congregations maintain high levels of responsiveness to individuals and their suggestions. Not only does participative planning encourage the initiatives of members, it also provides mechanisms by which members and leaders of the congregation can build upon one another's ideas. It provides the opportunity to develop common understandings and to agree upon major unifying themes which give a clear sense of direction to the congregation. Those major themes help to provide the unity that enables considerable diversity to exist creatively within the body.

Ministering congregations do differ from other congregations in the way they structure their planning activities. The predominant method of planning in all Presbyterian congregations is through session committees where groups of elders make plans which they bring to the whole session for approval. Ministering congregations are likely to expand those session committees beyond the elders themselves. They include members of the congregation as well, and even persons who have not yet united with the church. Elders often serve as chairpersons but that is not always the case. Getting the right person for the job is more important. Ministering congregations are also much less likely to leave the planning to the pastor and staff.

The Planning Process

There are several congregations in which participative planning has made a decisive contribution to the development of partnership in ministry. Their approaches to planning have several things in common.

1. *They have done a mission study.* Over an extended period of time they have involved a large number of people in Biblical and theological reflection on the mission of the church of Jesus Christ in general and of their congregation in particular. We have examined this in Chapter 2.

2. *They have developed a mission statement.* This is the product of the mission study. In brief it tells who they understand themselves to be and what they feel called to do. It serves as the major focus of all other planning. In one congregation "The Call," as it was named, was the result of three years' work by officers and staff. Another congregation developed its "Confession of Faith" over a period of a year. It is subject to annual review and revision, if necessary. (See Appendix 5.)

3. *They have defined several related objectives or direction statements.* This may well involve an extended process of evaluation of all existing programs in order to define specifically the kinds of things that the congregation should be doing in the light of their mission statement.

4. *They engage in an annual planning process.* In some organized way they define more specifically what they intend to do during the ensuing year. They develop specific action steps and program proposals.[29] Many congregations have members who are accustomed to planning for their work, whether it be to make lesson plans for a class, to plan for a small business venture, or to participate in elaborate planning processes in large corporations. Each congregation will need to discover its own ways to plan. Above all, give ample opportunities for members themselves to make suggestions. Keep them informed and involved.

A Forceful Collegial Style

To climb down off the pedestal and to develop collegial patterns of ministry takes a strong leader, not a weak one. Common stereotypes leave a lingering doubt in the back of many minds. Is not the sharing of leadership a sign of weakness? If people know where they are going and what they are doing and if they have deep convictions about it, will they not be directive in their style of leadership rather than collaborative? Our answer is no.

It is true that in two or three of the ministering congregations change toward partnership in ministry was initiated by pastors who have strong personalities with vigorous directive styles of relating to people. One has even been referred to as a "benevolent despot." It is even possible that without that type of directive leadership during the early stages of change, shared ministry may never have taken place in those congregations. One of these pastors had such a compelling dream of the ministry of the laity in the world and such a passion for the church to involve itself in corporate social change that others were carried along with his passion and enthusiasm. However, both he and his session realized how important it was to build a caring community within the congregation. So they called an associate pastor who was particularly gifted as a healer, who made people feel accepted, and who built community. Through him they learned to minister to one another. Later he succeeded the original pastor and further developed the strong participatory style that now characterizes the congregation. How does one sort out the contribution of each? The congregation today would not be what it is without each of them and without both types of strong leadership exerted in tandem and in sequence.

There is no evidence that such a sequence has been necessary in other congregations where change has taken place. There is ample evidence, however, that the pastors of ministering congregations are indeed strong leaders who have the skills of involving others in ministry.

Elders in ministering congregations were much more likely than elders in other congregations to say that their pastor gives strong leadership in developing the program of the church. They characterize their pastors as persons with aggressive enthusiasm, perseverance, boldness, willingness to risk, openness, and honesty. The strength of their leadership is focused, not on achieving their own will but on the growth and effectiveness of their people. They are servant leaders. They understand and practice the meaning of our Lord's words, "He who is greatest among you shall be your servant."

CHAPTER 8

Coming Alive

> The wind blows wherever it wishes; you hear
> the sound it makes, but you do not know
> where it comes from or where it is going. It
> is like that with everyone who is born of the
> Spirit.
>
> (John 3:8, TEV)

So you want your church to become a ministering congregation. What can be done to help it happen? How does a congregation come alive?

The question is simple, but the answer complex. Certainly there are some things that a congregation can do, but there is no miraculous fountain from which a congregation can drink that guarantees new vitality.

The Mystery of Coming Alive

It is relatively easy to observe ministering congregations and describe what they are like. We have reported what we have seen and heard. We have been told why they do what they are doing. Clear and recurring patterns have been identified, summarized, and illustrated. But it is not so easy to say what any particular congregation ought to do in order to grow into a responsive people of God.

Description is not difficult. Prescription is difficult and dangerous! There are too many variables. Cause and effect may *seem* obvious. If they do, the diagnosis is probably faulty. Any

157

given situation is almost infinitely complex. Actions taken in one congregation which seem to produce certain results may not be productive in another. A group of persons who gather for any purpose constitutes a complicated entity. The dynamic interrelationships between different parts of the body are not always predictable. Mystery abounds in every human interaction.

An even greater mystery is present whenever God interacts with his people. No matter how much we understand the way people relate to one another in social systems, no matter how well we understand God's revelation in Jesus Christ, there is a mystery about the church of Jesus Christ.

"The wind blows wherever it wishes; you hear the sound it makes, but you don't know where it comes from or where it is going. It is like that with everyone who is born of the Spirit." It is the grace of God and the mysterious movement of God's Spirit that calls out the people of God. There is no question about it. Yet it is equally clear that we have a part in the work of the Spirit in our lives. At the very least, we must be responsive to the Spirit, be open to God's purposes for his people. When Yahweh had persuaded Israel to move out into the desert, the armies of Pharaoh were behind them and the Red Sea was in front of them. Facing certain disaster, they cried out to the Lord in fear and anguish. "Why are you crying out for help?" the Lord asked Moses. "Tell the people to move forward." (Ex. 14:15, TEV.) We can count on God's help, but we must do our part, we must respond.

Paying the Price

If we want to become a ministering congregation, are we willing to pay the price? When our Lord was about to heal the man beside the pool of Bethzatha, he asked a *strange* question. "Do you want to get well?" (John 5:6, TEV.) Why wouldn't he want to get well? He had been crippled for thirty-eight years and healing would place that man back into a world where he would have to take responsibility for himself. He would have to pay a price for getting well. Are we deeply enough committed to becoming God's active people that we are willing to pay the price?

Members in ministering congregations were asked what advice they would give to people of another church who said they wanted to become a ministering congregation. Among those answers was this challenge:

"Before you do anything else you've got to ask: 'What's your commitment? Are you really committed to doing something like that? Are you willing to give time and money; willing to enlist others to work with you; willing to give up your weekends once in a while; willing to give up your evenings? How hard are you willing to work?' If you get an affirmative answer to all those questions, then you can start talking about planning. Without that, you might as well forget it!"

I. UNDERSTANDING AND ACCEPTING CHANGE

As we begin to think about strategies for bringing about growth in a congregation, we must think about change. What blocks change, and what facilitates it? To what extent is change within the church conditioned by the society within which the church finds itself? And how can an understanding of the complex forces of change help us to minimize undesirable side effects from changes we seek to introduce into congregational life?

Fear of Change

It is not hard to understand why most of us resist change. Familiar ways are comfortable. Even when they are not, we realize that growth can be painful. We resist change because we fear what change will do to us. In other words, fear is one important source of the pain we face when we contemplate change. Fear may drive us to seek solutions in increased activity.

John Harris tells of a once successful congregation that found itself in new circumstances. Membership dropped, ethusiasm waned. The congregation was in trouble and knew it. When the leaders saw the danger signals they went to work. They reorganized, set goals, developed new programs and new formats for their worship services. They revised their church school curriculum, developed small groups of various kinds, tried different patterns of adult classes. Though all of this was well planned, the congregation failed to recover vitality. Why? Because of fear. They feared failure, fiscal collapse, and change in their ways of administering the church. Significant change failed to take place.

The leaders were committed to careful planning, but fear prevented them from discovering what their problems really were. They did not analyze the forces in their situation that might block the changes they considered to be desirable. Harris concludes: "Messiah's leaders were not paralyzed by problems, but by the fear of the anxiety they would feel if they faced them. . . . Change in all forms was frightening because it was unpredictable and potentially divisive. Because of this they focused their energies inward and created more and more programs on the assumption that 'program production' was the right remedy for every congregational ill."[30]

Love Casts Out Fear

Harris quotes John MacMurray: "There are two, and I think only two, emotional attitudes through which human life can be radically determined. They are love and fear. Love is the positive principle of life, while fear is the death principle in us."[31] Harris says: "Fear shuts down spontaneity, and most importantly turns us away from others and in upon ourselves. Fear drowns out our capacities for life." Love, on the other hand, "stirs us into active interaction with the world around us." It expresses itself "in actions of reaching out, of openness, of compassion, of challenging bad traditions, of persisting in the face of obstacles, of imagining, of being alive to the human world in which we move."[32]

Christian faith calls us to face our fears, not to avoid them. We will have misfortune, fear, and anxiety. But if we are "truly alive" and "accept the fear and not avoid it, it will lose its power to destroy" our lives.[33] The argument is fine as far as it goes. It would be much stronger if Harris made explicit the relationship between fear and love in Christian faith. "Perfect love casts out fear." The active, accepting, and reconciling love of the living Christ at work in our lives destroys the power of fear and frees us to accept change. We can learn to accept change because the one who loves us will be waiting for us in new and different circumstances, just as he is with us in our present situation.

What Facilitates Change?

Where change has come about in ministering congregations the joyous power of love in action has made it possible. Fears must be faced. But unless they are faced within the context of powerful personal love, redemptive hope will not emerge on the other side of fear. To cast out the demons without a new and redeeming presence is to invite seven worse devils to come in.

What facilitates change? The power of God's love at work in God's caring community.

The Context of Change

To what extent is change within the church conditioned by the society around it? The church is always interacting with its environment. Not only is the church in the world; the world is in the church as well.

Looking again at the Biblical image of the church as the body of Christ, we are now affirming that the growing discipline of ecology has something to say to us as we contemplate change in the church. The intricate systems within the body —the digestive and circulatory, for example—must maintain a delicate balance for the body to function. There are also intricate ecological systems outside the body that affect its life as well. We are learning the painful lesson that change at any point in our environment affects us all. The church also influences its environment. The cultural values of church members may block or facilitate growth and change. To a great extent they condition the way a congregation is likely to react to potential change. Certainly cultural factors must be taken into account in planning a strategy for change in a congregation.

The Power of Purpose

We are not completely dependent upon our environment. The interdependence of the church with culture does not finally determine the outcome. Robert Worley speaks of *purposeful interdependency*. He says: "We are not *just* interdependent, being influenced at will by the forces around us. Purpose, the purpose of the church, can bring a new dimension into our necessary, unavoidable relationships. This phenomenon of *purposeful interdependency* introduces a hopeful note into church life."[34]

Harris also reminds us of faith's determining role: "We are responsible for what we do in the face of change and what we do is the result of what we believe—a matter of faith."[35]

II. Developing a Strategy

In considering possible strategies for change, where do we begin? Which approach is most likely to be productive? In what sequence should plans be developed? What role in the change process should the pastor play? How do lay leaders play their part?

Where Do We Begin?

Where do we begin? The answer is deceptively simple. We begin where we are. Actually we cannot begin anywhere else. It is imperative to understand the starting point. We need to know in what ways the congregation already is like a ministering congregation. Is the ministry of the whole people of God an important theme in its life? Does it have a clear sense of mission and identity? Do people understand the meaning of grace in their relationships with one another? What opportunities are there for small face-to-face experiences? Are leaders identifying, cultivating, and linking the gifts of people with opportunities for ministry? Is partnership between pastor and session and members a reality?

How much readiness is there for change? Do members fear it or are they eagerly waiting for it? Is there a desire to be involved in ministry? How large a core of leaders is committed to partnership in ministry? Is the pastor ready to change his or her style of ministry? Is the session prepared to share power? Are there enough key persons with influence in the congregation whose commitments to shared ministry are strong enough for them to be willing to work at it?

Answers to these questions should suggest the best strategy.

Taking Stock of Where You Are

One tool for making a careful analysis of where you are is the Ministry Survey found in Appendix 1. This consists of the most discriminating questions used in the Lay Ministry Questionnaire. Pastors can compare their answers with themes developed in this book. Elders can compare their answers with the answers of their pastor. The comparison can help answer two questions: In what ways is our congregation *already like* those congregations? And, In what ways would we *like it to be more like* those congregations? The same exercise could be used in a retreat with all the church officers, or with a larger group of members. Out of this analysis may come increased clarity on what a strategy for the congregation might be.

Many congregations have found a Mission Study to be a fruitful approach. This is a systematic examination of the community, the membership, the constituency, the congregation's goals and program to determine what it is already doing, and to chart its course into the future.

Whether or not one uses one of these approaches, or some others, it is important to think carefully about the total situation within the congregation, and within the community.

Which Themes Are Essential?

Which of the themes covered in the preceding chapters are most crucial for becoming ministering congregations? Most congregations in the study combine a large number of the characteristics described here. But not all of the themes are present in all the congregations. Some ideas that work exceedingly well in one situation would be highly inappropriate in another. However, *some* combination of *many* of these themes seems essential to the development of a ministering congregation.

What Is the Best Sequence?

There appears to be no particular sequence to introducing the various elements of a strategy. Many of the themes will need to become a reality in relation to other themes. Several different strategic approaches will be suggested in the pages that follow. Some may mutually exclude others. But most of them might be combined in some way, depending upon the particular congregation and where it now finds itself. Therefore the order given below has no particular significance.

III. THE PASTOR'S PLACE IN A STRATEGY

In a majority of cases the transition from a pastor-centered ministry to a shared ministry is initiated by the pastor. The pastor's determination to develop a partnership in ministry coupled with a particular style of leadership is crucial. Certainly if a pastor wants to block partnership in ministry, it is almost inconceivable that anything can happen. This is not to say that initiative for shared ministry cannot come from lay leaders. They also play a *crucial* role, but less frequently is it an initiatory role. If a lay leader or church member catches the vision of a ministering congregation, an early step should be to talk it over with the pastor. Pastors may be much more open to partnership in ministry than any member imagines. Find out how your pastor feels. Many pastors would welcome this expression of interest. They may even be waiting for the right moment to get others involved and may welcome allies in the cause. If they show some interest, ask how you can help make your dream become a reality. A lasting move toward shared ministry must have the unqualified support of the pastor, so patience and perseverance at the outset can prove to be worth the effort.

Words of Caution and Encouragement

The descriptions of pastors in ministering congregations found in this book may produce two undesirable effects:

They may lay a heavy burden on any pastor who assumes that every pastor should have all the qualities summarized here. That would be a cruel and impossible ideal. No person could possibly combine all these characteristics. Composites are helpful only as clues. Clues are helpful only as stimuli for selecting a very few areas in which pastors may wish to change their styles of ministry.

Congregations, on the other hand, may be tempted to use the composite picture of pastors as an excuse, saying, "The reason our members are not more involved in ministry is that our pastor is not like this or like that." If mutual ministry means anything, it means that no one person can be given the blame or the credit for the way things are. Rather, the task is for pastor, officers, and members together to take the findings of this study and discover how they may prove helpful in their relationship of *mutual* responsibility.

Do I Dare Share Power?

A principal reason for hesitancy in sharing power may be the pastor's own concern about the consequences. Is it worth the risk? If one tries and fails, what then? What do you do if you feel insecure about sharing power? How can such hesitancy be overcome?

The principle of taking small achievable steps, which seems to work so well with the cultivation of gifts in ministering congregations, may work for the pastor too. Success in one small step gives courage to take another. That in turn gives even more confidence. A hesitant pastor might decide on several small ways to give lay leaders greater responsiblity. Each step will provide some experience in sharing ministry without taking an undue amount of risk. Each success will give the additional courage to take a larger step. Also the thrill of seeing others come alive will provide additional motivation. In place of the satisfactions that come from doing a good job will come the even greater satisfactions from helping others to do so.

This is the way that many have learned to share leadership. A few pastors have such high levels of personal security that they quite naturally share leadership with others. Others have such low levels of personal security that they probably never could share power under any circumstances. Most of us have enough personal security that we can learn a participatory style of leadership if we are willing to try. My own natural inclinations are toward a directive style of leadership. Through sensitization, training, and experience my greatest satisfaction now comes from sharing in the development and increased effectiveness of colleagues. It can be done!

Acquiring the Needed Skills

Participatory leadership does require skill, whether natural or acquired. How does a pastor get those skills? Conversations with three different pastors of ministering congregations will illustrate. Their education and experiences were quite different. We will call them Jack, Jim, and Joe.

Jack developed his open style of working with his parishioners through role models within his own family. His seminary education did little to prepare him for it.

"My seminary taught you to be aloof. It was never articulated, but there was a kind of breeding that raises up austere people who maintain their distance and their authority. I feel that I am pastor and leader of the church, but that is not maintained by distance-keeping games. Accessibility is something I guess I picked up from my dad, and from my grandfather, and from my great-grandfather. All of them are pastors."

Jim, on the other hand, ascribes his partnership style to the influence of two of his seminary professors, both of whom had counseling background.

"My attitudes developed with George Jackson. He turned you loose in freedom from the start of your classes with him. We set our own grades. He helped develop the concept of being open and vulnerable. So also did Harry Jones. They built openness into all we did. They believed that the body of Christ is the laity. It is in that freedom that I am able to work as I do."

Joe is grateful for his seminary education, but found that he needed much more. He has been engaged in an extended series of continuing education events.

"My seminary gave us a good Biblical education. But they didn't give us a clue that we would shock people when we started working in a parish. They gave us no tools for conflict management. One of my most significant continuing education experiences was a Young Pastors Seminar. Since then I have had training in transactional analysis, pastoral care, and supervision."

Continuing Education Is Vital

Pastors of ministering congregations are actively engaged in continuing education. Many of them have taken advanced degrees in nontheological fields as well.

Appendix 6 shows the subjects of study in which pastors of ministering congregations engaged beyond the basic seminary course. Nearly two thirds of the courses taken were in subjects related to various forms of human relations skills. These pastors have been working in such areas as pastoral care, counseling, clinical pastoral education, change agent skills, sensitivity training, transactional analysis, community organization, education, and management.

How does a pastor acquire the perspectives and skills required to develop partnership in ministry? Apparently this comes as a consequence of a continual pattern of professional growth over a number of years. It comes through maintaining a balance between the Biblical and the theological disciplines on the one hand and those disciplines that are person-oriented. In the postseminary phase of preparation a heavier emphasis seems to be needed on the latter, but without neglecting the former. Without such an emphasis, it is highly doubtful that most pastors can be adequately equipped to share ministry with the people in their congregations.

What Is That in Your Hand?

If continuing education is to be of maximum value, it needs to be goal-oriented and to grow out of a careful appraisal of the participant's professional strengths and weaknesses. What personal and professional resources does one already have? How well developed are they? What else does one need in order to be more effective?

The Pastoral Performance Profile, developed by the Vocation Agency,[36] is a tool designed to help the pastor make such a self-assessment. It grows out of a study of what pastors actually do in the pastoral ministry.

Pastors who wish to assess their performance work with a neighboring pastor and a lay leader from their own congregation. They gather specific illustrations of the things they *actually do* in relation to each activity. Thus pastors may determine that they are "highly competent" in performing certain functions and "competent" or "below standard" in performing other functions. The resulting profile provides specific information on which to determine what *changes they want* in their ministries. This in turn gives them a relatively objective basis for planning professional growth activities and continuing education.

Another way to assess one's strength is through counseling in one of the several interdenominational career centers that have been established in different parts of the country. Among the methods they use is a Motivated Abilities Analysis instrument in which clients are asked to recall achievements throughout their lifetime. An achievement is defined as something you did that gave you a sense of satisfaction because it used the best that is in you. The client is helped to analyze the achievements to determine what characteristics contributed to each of them. As patterns are identified, clients get a clearer picture of their own strengths, and of the kinds of things that give them a sense of fulfillment.

Learning to Listen

If such analysis reveals that *learning to listen* should get high priority, a pastor has a specific learning objective: to seek out opportunities that teach others how to listen effectively. Training in counseling or interviewing might be indicated. It is possible to learn to listen actively and empathetically if one is willing to work at it. Robert Greenleaf suggests that "a non-servant who wants to be a servant might become a *natural* servant through a long and arduous discipline of learning to listen. . . . I have seen enough remarkable transformations in people who have been trained to listen to have some confidence in this approach."[37]

Learning to Delegate and to Supervise

Pastors whose need to control everything is interfering with their effectiveness might enroll in management workshops. Here they could develop skills in delegating responsibility, in supervision, or in use of Management by Objectives. Good supervisors can give considerable autonomy to those with whom they work. It is neither necessary to abdicate one's own responsibility nor dominate others as they carry out their tasks.

Learning to Share Vulnerability

Pastors who find it difficult to admit their shortcomings might participate in various human relations training events. Many are designed to help participants feel more comfortable about expressing their feelings through colleague relationships or with a Koinonia group.

A staff member of one of the ministering congregations was

asked what he would do differently if he were to go back to the
congregation from which he came. He replied that he would
develop the same, kind of collegiate relationship with two
neighboring pastors as he now had with other members of his
staff. He would share his real feelings with them, and the three
of them would hold each other accountable for getting lay
people involved in ministry. Harris puts it well when he says,
"Only pastors who struggle to become more free as persons in
the company of others are free to assist others search for freedom."[38]

Learning to Seek Complementarity

Pastors who clearly understand their strengths and shortcomings can work with the lay leaders to design a shared
ministry which capitalizes on those strengths and minimizes
those weaknesses. If the pastoral nominating committee has
done its work well, it has chosen the pastor because of particular strengths that are needed by the congregation. Others on
the session can be responsible for areas in which the pastor is
less gifted.

IV. THE SESSION'S ROLE

If partnership in ministry is impossible without the full cooperation of the pastor, it is equally impossible without the complete commitment of a core of lay leaders. The place to begin
will normally be with the session. Let us summarize what this
might involve:

1. *Discuss the meaning of ministry.* Do you agree that ministry is the work of all church members? What does that mean
for the ministry of the pastor? the ministries of elders? Discuss
the different themes developed in this book.

2. *Covenant to share ministry.* If you agree that ministry is
the work of all church members, make a covenant with one
another. Determine that pastor, elders, and members will become partners in ministry. Together discover what that

means. Make the changes in the way you work so that partnership becomes a reality. It will take time to work out the details, but agree on the goal.

3. *Analyze your present situation.* Use the Ministry Survey to discover where your congregation already is a ministering congregation, and where you want to become more like such congregations. What changes in session leadership style are needed?

4. *Learn and pray together.* Set aside time in session meetings to know each other as persons and to share your spiritual pilgrimages. Study the Bible and other books together. Pray together.

5. *Share your experiences.* To understand more fully the meaning of ministry, share your experiences of ministering to others and of *receiving ministry from* others. The latter can be especially productive for persons who are used to being in leadership positions.

6. *Clarify your expectations of one another.* In the light of your understanding of shared ministry, and of the gifts each person is given, clarify your role in the leadership of the church. What sort of leadership role and style do you expect of the pastor? How can your pastor help the elders become more effective ministers? Discuss your expectations for the role and style of the ministry of elders. How can the whole session help members in their ministries? Clarifying expectations is especially important at the beginning of a new pastoral relationship, but it should be repeated periodically thereafter.

7. *Delegate responsibility.* Assign authority to commissions or committees that are broadly representative of the congregation. Share your power.

8. *Give others an opportunity.* Invite suggestions from the whole congregation. Find ways to be responsive to any reasonable initiative. Affirm and recognize such initiative. Let programming grow out of the gifts and initiatives of the members and constituency.

9. *Continue your own education.* Lay leaders, like pastors, must grow in their understanding of faith and of their responsibilities as leaders. Like pastors, they need constantly to

sharpen their skills. Ministering congregations are much more active in developing programs for training lay leaders than are other congregations.

V. ELEMENTS IN A STRATEGY

Throughout this book different strategic approaches have been suggested. Some of those possibilities are summarized here.

A. *Getting a Sense of Direction*

1. *Rediscover your Biblical roots.* Through churchwide study of the book of The Acts, or major Biblical themes, think about the nature of the church and the calling of every Christian.

2. *Define the mission of your congregation.* Conclude your study by developing a statement that includes such things as: What is the essence of the gospel? What is the meaning of ministry? What is the mission of the church? What is your unique calling as a people of God in your particular place at this particular time? What are the needs and opportunities of your community?

3. *Enlist the ministers.* Share your vision of the congregation's unique mission. Call people to their ministries. Develop enthusiasm for important commitments.

4. *Hold high expectations for your members.* Believe that they will want to involve themselves in ministry. Give opportunities for them to do so and communicate your confidence in them.

B. *Strategies with a Sharp Focus*

1. *Concentrate on a few contagious multipliers.* Identify potential spiritual leaders. Cultivate those who will help others to get involved in ministry. Form a Koinonia group with them. Disciple them. Give them experience with others who model

acceptance, openness, and caring love. Equip them to be equippers of others. Give priority to making ministries effective.

2. *Widen the circles of influence.* Start with the contagious multipliers as a core group. Work outward in ever-widening circles. Develop their leadership skills. Put them to work with others. Give them leadership responsibilities in training others. Let them recruit their own Koinonia group members. Affirm their ministries and give them whatever support they need.

3. *Focus on new members.* Especially in congregations with high rates of turnover, new members provide the greatest opportunity to make a difference in the life of the congregation. Expect great things from them. Get them involved in Inquirers groups. Out of Inquirers groups develop Koinonia groups.

4. *Work toward a tipping point.* It takes time and infinite patience to develop a ministering congregation. As the circle enlarges of those who are committed to ministry, more resources become available to get others involved. At some point, a large core of enthusiastic members may begin to turn the tide.

5. *Facilitate face-to-face fellowship.* Work on community building. Provide as many different opportunities as possible for people to form intimate relationships with others around things that matter to their spiritual growth and involvement in ministry. Use existing structures. Get the session, committees, and task groups involved in sharing as persons with one another and in providing mutual support. Let people learn to minister in their natural church work settings. Encourage a wide variety of small groups.

C. Strategies That Involve People

1. *Visit a ministering congregation.* Learn more about ministering congregations by visiting one of them. Send your pastor and the lay leaders for a weekend to a congregation that has the characteristics you seek. Ask your team to observe,

participate in their activities, and talk with key persons who can help you understand what they do and why. Ministering congregations will be glad to share what they can.

2. *Invite a team from a ministering congregation.* A number of ministering congregations consider it one of their ministries to help other congregations come alive. They are eager to share what they have discovered. The Pleasant Lake congregation has what they call a Macedonian Ministry. Once or twice a year they will go to another church to conduct a retreat for church officers or for the congregation as a whole. Grace Church has a similar ministry of lay leader training and congregational renewal.

3. *Serve on presbytery committees.* Several of the ministering congregations have found that one important way to involve members in ministry is through participation in presbytery committees. They have gained understandings of important issues, and deeper commitments to do something about them. In turn, they have awakened the concern of others within the congregation.

4. *Share in ecumenical ministries.* Several ministering congregations are involved in ministries within the community which are carried out through ecumenical agencies. Such cooperative approaches provide a broader base for social service, community organization, or political action.

5. *Learn from others.* Mention has been made at several points of the significant influence that the Church of the Saviour has had on a number of congregations. Seek out the congregations that are alive and study what they are doing. Such outside stimuli can provide a valuable influence at crucial stages in a congregation's development.

6. *Involve the congregation in a major project.* Several ministering congregations look back upon some major project of ministry as the catalyst for their continual involvement in lay ministry. Sponsoring a refugee family can focus the resources of a congregation on a significant act of caring which is easily understood and in which most people can participate in some meaningful way. It provides opportunities to interpret the meaning of ministry. It directs attention upon a particular

family whom the congregation can get to know. It provides opportunities to work together in finding housing, gathering furniture, securing warm clothing, finding employment, teaching the family English or otherwise following them with love and support. It reinforces the importance of ministry as appreciation is expressed, and people feel that they have participated in something significant.

The Saint James congregation as part of their observance of Lent encouraged members to engage in at least one Lenten project. There were tables around the room where people could learn about, and sign up for, some form of Lenten service. One was to become involved in outreach to Spanish-speaking neighbors. Eight to ten persons signed up for that particular project. They interviewed key people in the Hispanic community. They visited in a few homes. As they got involved in understanding the community, they saw great need. They saw poor housing, broken windows, rats, cockroaches, barefoot children. Participants in the project found that they could not turn their backs on the needs. Out of the Lenten project grew the organization of a community center.

7. *Seek specific commitments in small packages.* Single events, study opportunities, and short-term service possibilities allow people to dip their toe into the water before taking the plunge. Give them a chance to get involved in a small way before you ask them to take on extensive projects.

8. *Recognize crises as natural points of entry.* Keep alert to the periods of crisis in the lives of individuals and of the congregation as a whole. Not only is that a time when people need the ministry of others, it is also a time when they can learn the meaning of ministry and grow as ministers themselves. During times of crisis people are actually aware of their own needs, and of their humanity. One pastor says: "Mission grows out of our own brokenness. Until you have been able to ask for help you are not ready for ministry."

9. *Capitalize on the interim between pastors.* Most congregations get anxious when they face a gap between the leaving of their pastor and the calling of a new one. This can indeed be a period of stress. But it can also provide an important opportu-

nity to strengthen lay leadership in the congregation. The pastor of one ministering congregation believes his people turned the corner to active involvement in lay ministry before he came. They were without a pastor for over a year and recognized their responsibility to *be* the church in new ways. When he began his pastorate with them, he was very careful to keep the reins of ministry in the hands of lay leaders who had assumed them before he came. An interim pastor who knows how to encourage partnership in ministry can make an important contribution in that direction.

D. Ongoing Tasks That Undergird Partnership

1. *Go on a perpetual treasure hunt.* Challenge members of the congregation to be good stewards of their giftedness. Emphasize the gifts of the Spirit. Focus on talents and potentials. Encourage and respond to initiatives. Take people and their ideas seriously. Develop gifts incrementally by stages. Match gifts to needs. Affirm people in their ministries.

2. *Develop adult growth opportunities.* Involve the members of the church in study and growth experiences. Biblical and theological reflection in a relational setting provides crucial undergirding to ministry. Develop programs that raise vision and sensitize persons to human needs and opportunities for ministry. Let preaching and worship experiences awaken the people to their calling to mission in a broken world. Integrate preaching themes with study and sharing in small groups. Encourage people to join task groups in specific ministry projects.

One session has developed its strategy around a School for Christian Living. They have called a minister of lay training and are developing a Discipleship Center. In these and other ways they have made clear to the whole congregation that they are serious about equipping lay people for their ministries.

3. *Ensure effective communication.* In talking with leaders of ministering congregations one is impressed with the crucial role that communication plays. People feel they know what is

happening. They know what the session is doing and why. They know what the pastor is doing. They sense that they are on the inside of something important rather than on the outside looking in.

And Having Done All?

How does a congregation come alive? Paradoxically, there is much that we can do, yet all is in God's hands. We must be born again, yet that birth is of the Spirit who is like the wind that blows where it wills.

Congregations come alive by sounding a clear call to ministry in which all members participate; by discovering grace as a way of life; by becoming a caring community and family of God; by renewal through face-to-face relationships; by using the gifts God has given; and by sharing power as partners.

There is much that a congregation can do to create a favorable climate within which partnership can grow. Yet it is the Spirit that gives life. It is the Spirit that moves in the hearts and minds of the people of God.

The Spirit's gifts to the pastors of ministering congregations is a style of ministry which awakens and cultivates the ministries of all God's people. Such gifts are received, not earned. They are the gifts the church must seek in those it calls to be its pastors. Yet each of these faithful servants has faithfully cultivated those gifts through careful preparation, through spiritual formation and ongoing professional development.

The Spirit's gifts to members of ministering congregations is an openness to the movement of that same Spirit in their lives, both as individuals and as the body of Christ. To be in ministry is to be a part of God's mission in the world: to discover God's will and do it. It is that gift of responsiveness to the will of God that congregations long for when they seek to become *Congregations Alive*!

For those who wish to use this book for study or discussion, a few questions and activities are outlined for each chapter. They are intended to be suggestive. Choose those which seem helpful or develop your own approach.

Chapter 1. A LOOK AT LIVING CONGREGATIONS

1. In what ways is your congregation already like the ministering congregations? How would you like it to be?

To answer these questions, ask each church officer to fill out the Ministry Survey (Appendix 1). Tabulate the results. Use the filmstrip *A Tale of Three Churches* to introduce the discussion. Compare your answers to those given in the filmstrip.

2. What ministries does your congregation now carry on? In what ministries do you think your congregation should be involved?

To answer these questions, study the list of ministries found in ministering congregations (Appendix 2). Consider which of these ministries you carry on as part of your own program; as part of an ecumenical partnership; through a community agency; or through individual ministries of members. Consider the needs for ministry within your congregation; within the community; within the nation or the world. What else should you be doing?

3. Share with one another your individual experiences of receiving ministry from someone else. What does that tell you about the meaning of ministry? What does that say about how you minister to others?

4. Plan an officers retreat, or set aside time in each regular meeting for study of this book, a chapter at a time.

Chapter 2. SOUNDING A CLEAR CALL

1. Study the Biblical images of the church described in this chapter or those in The Acts or Ephesians.

2. Write a corporate statement on the nature of the church and its mission. Let the pastor and each officer write separate statements. Discuss them and try to reach a consensus.

3. Write a corporate statement that defines the unique ministry of your congregation.

4. What can be done to help the members of your congregation capture a vision of lay ministry? Does your current program contribute to such a vision? What else might you be doing?

5. In what ways do you agree or disagree that the pastor's task is to prepare and sustain members in their ministries? If the pastor were to concentrate full attention on that task, what kinds of things the pastor now does would have to be done by lay leaders? Would such a shift be desirable or practical?

Chapter 3. DISCOVERING GRACE AS A WAY OF LIFE

1. What is the meaning of grace in the experience of your congregation? How would visitors and new members characterize the reception they receive in your congregation?

2. How far can you go in accepting people whose life-styles differ radically from yours? What is the relationship between individual and corporate moral standards and acceptance of persons who violate those standards?

3. What does your congregation expect of its members? What impact do those expectations have on the level of commitment of its members? In the light of the experience of ministering congregations, what changes, if any, should you make in your expectations?

4. What are the relative advantages, risks, and cautions involved in a pastor sharing his or her vulnerability with parishioners?

Chapter 4. BECOMING A CARING COMMUNITY

1. In what ways is your congregation a caring community? How might you encourage the development of koinonia? What forces favor such growth? What are the blocking forces? Decide on a plan of action for the coming year.

2. In what ways does worship in your congregation symbolize partnership? How does it involve members in preparing and leading worship? What changes does your discussion suggest?

3. To what extent are members of your congregation involved in service in presbytery, in the community, or otherwise outside the congregation itself? Make a survey and plan to affirm that service personally or liturgically. What more might you do to encourage such service?

4. Has it been your experience that "cared for people will care for people"? What, if anything, is wrong with that formulation? In what ways is caring happening in your congregation? How might it happen with more members?

Chapter 5. RENEWAL THROUGH RELATIONSHIPS

1. Discuss the relative advantages or disadvantages of expecting every new member to participate in an Inquirers group.

2. Plan a strategy for experimenting with Koinonia groups.

3. Arrange to correspond with or visit a congregation that has an active group life. Report your experiences to the session and discuss their implications for the work of your congregation.

4. What possibilities and problems do you see in a Parish Care program similar to those described in this chapter?

5. How do you react to the idea of the pastor or a church officer consciously modeling ministry to members of the congregations?

Chapter 6. USING THE GIFTS GOD HAS GIVEN

1. How much emphasis do you give to the gifts of the Spirit in your teaching, preaching, counseling, and group life?

2. In recruiting leadership, do you believe people will want to use their gifts if given an opportunity to do so? What do you really believe about members' readiness to serve? What implications does that have for enabling the gifts of the members?

3. To what extent do programs of your congregation grow out of the initiatives of members? How might you be more responsive to their concerns, dreams, and program ideas?

4. Should you give primary attention to recruiting people to carry out programs others have planned, or to developing opportunities for members to make creative use of their gifts and to fulfill their potential for ministry? To what extent are these approaches compatible?

5. How can you identify the gifts of the members of your congregation and match those gifts to possibilities for ministry? In what ways should you take initiative in asking people to accept certain responsibilities?

6. If the gifts of people can best be cultivated through small achievable steps, what implications does this have for work with members of the congregation?

Chapter 7. SHARING POWER AS PARTNERS

1. What expectations do pastor and church officers have for each other? Use the Pastoral Expectations Inventory (Appendix 4). Define your mutual expectations in a covenant which you can review, revise, and renew every year or two. Interpret the results of your work to members of the congregation.

2. Have the pastor and church officers fill out the Ministry Survey (Appendix 1). Compare your answers and reach a consensus on the role and leadership style of pastor and church officers.

3. Discuss what partnership in ministry might mean in your congregation. If pastor and officers were to develop a true partnership, what would you do differently? What things in your congregation facilitate or block partnership between pastor and members?

4. How can you come down off your pedestals as pastor and decision makers?

5. Decide upon specific ways to disperse decision-making, encourage initiative, and secure participation of church members in planning.

Chapter 8. COMING ALIVE

1. What new emphases might be most productive of new life in your congregation?

2. What changes in your congregation have been suggested by your study? Agree on the most important changes you would like to initiate.

3. Develop a strategy for introducing to your congregation the changes you have identified. What forces favor these changes or block them? How can you minimize the blocking forces and encourage the favorable forces? How can you be responsive to the Holy Spirit in making these plans?

4. In what ways can the leadership of your congregation encourage the growth of mutual trust and love among leaders and within the membership so as to create a climate in which change is possible?

5. Develop a plan of action for the coming year based upon your study of this book.

APPENDIX 1

MINISTRY SURVEY

The following questions are designed to help pastors and officers think together about the meaning and practice of ministry in their congregations. Each person answers the questions independently of others. Then one person tabulates the answers. A comparison of the tabulated results can lead to a fruitful discussion.

1. The word "ministry" is used with different meanings. Beside each statement place a number that best represents the extent of your agreement with the statement, as follows:

   1 Strongly Agree
   2 Agree
   3 Agree and Disagree
   4 Disagree
   5 Strongly Disagree

————A. Ministry is the special work of the pastor which serves the spiritual needs of the congregation (preaching, Bible teaching, pastoral calling, etc.).

————B. Ministry is the work shared in by pastors and elders which serves members of the congregation and their spiritual needs.

————C. Ministry is the work shared in by the whole congregation which serves the people of the congregation.

————D. Ministry includes serving people of the community outside the congregation such as visiting prisoners, volunteering for community service projects, or serving on the boards of community organizations.

————E. Ministry includes corporate action by the church to change unjust economic or political conditions of life (such as a task force to deal with issues related to the disparity between rich and poor nations).

————F. Ministry includes the ways a member lives out his or her faith in relation to family, friends, and neighborhood.

————G. Ministry includes the ways a member lives out his or her faith in his or her occupation.

2. To what extent does each of the following statements accurately describe your congregation? Beside each statement place a number that best represents your answer, as follows:

   1 Very much like my congregation
   2 Somewhat like my congregation
   3 Only a little like my congregation
   4 Not at all like my congregation
   5 Don't know

————A. Members have a clear sense of the congregation's purpose.

————B. Pastors and lay leaders share leadership as genuine partners.

————C. Members know that the church has high expectations for their commitment to and accountability for service.

185

———D. Members actively serve in the community.

———E. Members actively participate in evangelistic activities.

———F. Members pray together in many different times and places about common concerns.

———G. Members are involved in the work of the church as soon as they unite with the church, if not before.

———H. Members may choose many ways to serve.

———I. Members are challenged in specific ways to participate in community activities or organizations.

———J. Pastor(s) invite the sharing of joys and concerns before offering the pastoral prayer during Sunday worship.

———K. Members frequently minister to one another's needs.

———L. There are many small groups or other face-to-face opportunities for study, prayer, and mutual ministry.

———M. Members feel that the congregation is like a warm, caring family.

———N. Members take initiative in identifying needs and proposing ways to serve.

3. There are many ways in which pastors carry on their work. At different times they may give more or less emphasis to different aspects of ministry. Beside each statement place a number that best represents the relative priority which you feel the pastor of your congregation gives to that way of working, as follows:

        1 Very high priority
        2 High priority
        3 Low priority
        4 Very low priority
        5 No opinion/don't know

———A. Focuses attention on issues outside the congregation.

———B. Inspires and motivates members to be involved in service in the community.

———C. Frequently communicates the importance and the possibilities of ministry by church members.

———D. Identifies and encourages the use of members' gifts and talents.

———E. Interprets Biblical and theological perspectives on current issues.

———F. Listens to people and responds to their needs with caring love.

———G. Serves as a facilitator and provides resources to members in their ministries.

———H. Shares his or her humanity in specific ways.

———I. Develops confidence and feelings of self-worth in the church members.

———J. Asks people to do only what he or she would do.

———K. Clearly articulates a dream or goal for the congregation.

———L. Has a clear sense of his or her own appropriate roles in relation to the roles of church officers and members.

————M. Provides strong leadership in developing the program of the church.

————N. Responds to the program ideas of others and helps them to implement them.

4. How much help in living a life of service to others (at home, at work, in the community or in the church) do you now receive from each of the following? Beside each statement place a number that best represents your best response to that statement:

        1 Very much
        2 Quite a lot
        3 Some
        4 Little
        5 None
        6 Not sure

————A. From Sunday worship services and sermons?

————B. From fellowship with other church members?

————C. From small study groups and prayer?

————D. From personal Bible study and prayer?

————E. From the way other church members love and accept me as I am?

————F. From the way my pastor loves and accepts me as I am?

————G. From the inspiration of my pastor as a model of Christian service?

————H. From the way others in my congregation express their belief in my ability to serve?

————I. From the work of the Holy Spirit in our congregation?

————J. From appreciation I receive when I have served?

APPENDIX 2

TYPES OF MINISTRY ENGAGED IN BY 50 PERCENT
OR MORE OF THE MINISTERING CONGREGATIONS

(Types of ministry are listed below in rank order. The most frequent type of activity is listed first)

RANK

A. Counseling Services

B. Hospital Visitation

C. Food Pantries

D. Senior Citizens Programs

E. Crisis Ministries

F. Youth Recreation

G. Intergenerational Programs

H. Evangelistic Visitation

I. Hospital Volunteer Service

J. Hunger Programs

K. Clothing Closet

L. Parenting Classes

M. Elderly Transportation

N. Nursery School

O. Singles Ministry

P. Alcoholics Anonymous

Q. Foreign Student Hospitality

R. Community Organization

S. Justice Educational Programs

T. Meals on Wheels

APPENDIX 3

ROLE CONFLICT
Significant Differences Between Pastors and Elders
In Response to 62 Questions

	Presbyterian Panel		Ministering Congregations	
	#	%	#	%
All 62 questions	54	87	27	44
14 Descriptions of congregations	9	64	3	21
14 Style priorities	13	93	2	14
28 Combined items	22	79	5	18

APPENDIX 4

PRIORITY RATING FORM FOR CONGREGATIONAL AND PASTORAL ACTIVITIES

Indicate the relative importance of the following activities
in your particular congregation and in the particular position below.

ACTIVITIES	Congregation's Priorities (Priority Rating for the Total Life and Ministry of the Congregation)			Pastoral Activity Priorities (Priority Rating for the Ministry of ―――― (position))		
	A Should get greatest emphasis (check from 5 to 10 items)	B	C Should get least emphasis (check from 5 to 10 items)	A Should get greatest emphasis (check from 5 to 10 items)	B	C Should get least emphasis (check from 5 to 10 items)
1. Corporate Worship and Administration of Sacraments						
2. Proclamation of the Word						
3. Special Worship Services						
4. Spiritual Development of Members						
5. Congregational Home Visitation						
6. Hospital and Emergency Visitation						
7. Congregational Fellowship						
8. Counseling Services						
9. Evangelism						

10. Planning Congregational Life and Mission									
11. Involvement in Mission Beyond the Local Community									
12. Development of Educational Program									
13. Teaching Responsibilities									
14. Mission in the Local Community									
15. Ecumenical and Interfaith Activities									
16. Congregational Communication									
17. Administrative Leadership									
18. Stewardship and Commitment Program									
19. Financial and Property Management									
20. Evaluation of Program and Staff									
21. Responsibilities and Relationships with Presbytery and Other Judicatories									
22. Performance Appraisal									
23. Professional Growth	These three apply to the pastor or other staff person who is the focus of this study.								
24. Personal and Family Time									
25. _____									
26. _____									
27. _____									
28. _____									
29. _____									
30. _____									

APPENDIX 5

A CONGREGATION'S STATEMENT OF MISSION

"Confession of Faith"

We are a church which in recognizing the spiritual and human needs of our membership and our world believes that we can care as Jesus cared: for God, for each other, for the world, for self.

Because we care for God as Jesus cared, we shall encourage a growing commitment to God through a balanced involvement in worship, study, sharing, and serving.

Because as Christians we care for each other as Jesus cared for the disciples, we affirm that all persons, regardless of age, sex, race, life-style, political preference, or theological perspective, can lay claim to God's promise. Therefore we love, support, study with, pray for, reach out to, and celebrate each other through the life of the church, so that all in our reach will share God's promise.

Because we care for the world as Jesus cared, we shall go into the world with compassion for others: minimizing our material needs, seeking the way in matters of human justice, freedom and responsibility; involving all of us in service and sacrificial giving. Most of all we shall live as though the Kingdom of God were achieved in our midst rather than relying upon our planning and good works to achieve it.

Because I care for myself as Jesus cared for himself, I shall grow in my capacity to receive not only God's challenge but God's acceptance, finding new expressions for God's love in my major ministry of home, job, and community. Amen.

APPENDIX 6

AREAS OF STUDY BEYOND BASIC SEMINARY EDUCATION

	Percentage of Pastors (N=68)	
Biblical Study	72	
Theology	66	34% of all items
Evangelism	37	
Spiritual Formation	32	
Pastoral Care—Counseling	77	
Change Agent Skills	59	
Sensitivity Training	49	
Educational Skills	49	51% of all items
Community Organization	28	
Clinical Pastoral Education	27	
Transactional Analysis	22	
Administration—Management	66	11% of all items
Other	27	4% of all items

NOTES

1. Letty M. Russell, *The Future of Partnership* (Westminster Press, 1979), p. 133.
2. James C. Fenhagen, *Mutual Ministry: New Vitality for the Local Church* (Seabury Press, 1977).
3. Elizabeth O'Connor, *Journey Inward, Journey Outward* (Harper & Row, 1968), pp. ix–x.
4. Thomas W. Gillespie, in Ralph D. Bucy, ed., *The New Laity Between Churches and World* (Word Books, 1978), pp. 14–15.
5. Arnold B. Come, *Agents of Reconciliation* (Westminster Press, 1960), p. 48.
6. Gillespie, in Bucy, ed., *The New Laity Between Churches and World*, p. 25.
7. Hendrik Kraemer, *A Theology of the Laity* (Westminster Press, 1958), p. 140.
8. Henri Nouwen, *The Wounded Healer: Ministry in Contemporary Society* (Doubleday & Co., 1972), p. 93.
9. Ibid., p. 90.
10. Ibid., p. 73.
11. Ibid., p. 84.
12. Ibid., p. 38.
13. Ibid., p. 39.
14. Elizabeth O'Connor, *Call to Commitment: The Story of the Church of the Saviour, Washington, D.C.* (Harper & Row, 1963).
15. Robert C. Leslie, *Sharing Groups in the Church: An Invitation to Involvement* (Abingdon Press, 1971), p. 58.
16. John C. Harris, *Stress, Power and Ministry: An Approach to the Current Dilemmas of Pastors and Congregations* (Alban Institute, 1977), p. 14.
17. Dietrich Bonhoeffer, *Life Together* (Harper & Brothers, 1954), p. 23.
18. Leslie, *Sharing Groups in the Church*, p. 27.

19. Bonhoeffer, *Life Together,* pp. 26–27.

20. Chris Argyris, *Integrating the Individual and the Organization* (John Wiley & Sons, 1964).

21. Robert K. Greenleaf, *Servant Leadership: A Journey Into the Nature of Legitimate Power and Greatness* (Paulist Press, 1977), p. 7.

22. Russell, *The Future of Partnership,* pp. 71–72.

23. Harris, *Stress, Power and Ministry,* p. 59.

24. Greenleaf, *Servant Leadership,* p. 10.

25. Harris, *Stress, Power and Ministry,* p. 61.

26. For what to do about role ambiguity and conflict, see Donald P. Smith, *Clergy in the Cross Fire: Coping with Role Conflicts in the Ministry* (Westminster Press, 1973), pp. 81–138.

27. The Vocation Agency, The United Presbyterian Church in the U.S.A., *Pastoral Expectations Inventory,* in the Toward the Improvement of Ministry Series, 1976.

28. The Vocation Agency, The United Presbyterian Church in the U.S.A., *Pastoral Activities Index,* in the Toward the Improvement of Ministry Series, 1976.

29. For some suggestions on goal-setting and review, see Smith, *Clergy in the Cross Fire,* pp. 139ff.

30. Harris, *Stress, Power and Ministry,* pp. 33–34.

31. John MacMurray, *Freedom in the Modern World* (London: Faber & Faber, 1932, 1938), p. 27.

32. Harris, *Stress, Power and Ministry,* p. 40.

33. Ibid., p. 41.

34. Robert Worley, *Change in the Church: A Source of Hope* (Westminster Press, 1971), pp. 32–33.

35. Harris, *Stress, Power and Ministry,* pp. 28–29.

36. The Vocation Agency, The United Presbyterian Church in the U.S.A., *Pastoral Performance Profile,* in the Toward the Improvement of Ministry Series, 1976.

37. Greenleaf, *Servant Leadership,* p. 17.

38. Harris, *Stress, Power and Ministry,* p. 75.

OTHER RESOURCES

Chapter 2. SOUNDING A CLEAR CALL

Church Officer Pre-Ordination Curriculum Leaders Guide. Church Officer Development. Geneva Press, 1975.
Johnson, Robert Clyde, ed. *The Church and Its Changing Ministry.* Office of the General Assembly, The United Presbyterian Church in the U.S.A., 1961.
Paul, Robert S. *Ministry.* Wm. B. Eerdmans Publishing Co., 1965.

Chapter 4. BECOMING A CARING COMMUNITY

A Presbyterian Congregation at Worship. Unit 4: Continuing Education Series, Church Officer Development. Geneva Press, 1975.
The Session and Community Ministry. Unit 12: Continuing Education Series, Church Officer Development. Geneva Press, 1976.

Chapter 5. RENEWAL THROUGH RELATIONSHIPS

Barr, Browne. *The Well Church Book.* Seabury Press, 1976.

Chapter 6. USING THE GIFTS GOD HAS GIVEN

O'Connor, Elizabeth. *Eighth Day of Creation: Gifts and Creativity.* Word Books, 1971.
Recruiting and Utilizing the Abilities of Church Leaders. Unit 6: Continuing Education Series, Church Officer Development. Geneva Press, 1975.

Chapter 7. SHARING POWER AS PARTNERS

The Administrative Responsibility of the Session. Unit 11: Continuing Education Series, Church Officer Development. Geneva Press, 1976.
Smith, Donald P. *Clergy in the Cross Fire: Coping with Role Conflicts in the Ministry.* Westminster Press, 1973.

Chapter 8. COMING ALIVE

Adams, James R., and Hahn, Celia A. *Learning to Share the Ministry.* Alban Institute, 1975.

Anderson, James D., and Jones, Ezra Earl. *The Management of Ministry.* Harper & Row, 1978.

Hahn, Celia A., ed. *Patterns for Parish Development.* Seabury Press, 1974.

Hoge, Dean. *Division in the Protestant House.* Westminster Press, 1976.

The Session and Community Ministry. Unit 12: Continuing Education Series, Church Officer Development. Geneva Press, 1976.

Worley, Robert C. *Dry Bones Breathe!* Center for the Study of Church Organizational Behavior, 1978.